I am dedicating this recipe book to my sweet mom, who gave me the passion I have for recipe books and baking. I'm grateful for the patience she had with me, as a young girl on the farm, wanting to learn how to bake.

I miss you Mom.

About the Author

Joanne Marsh has been active in a nutritional supplement business since 1982. Her passion for studying nutrition has helped her to acquire knowledge on how nutrition affects the body. Along with guidance from a world-renowned physician/scientist, Mohamed Nasr, M.D., Cardiologist, Agronomist, a member of the American Board of Holistic Medicine, with 5 years of Research on Bioflavonoids; she has developed delicious, healthy, low-glycemic desserts, treats and more.

Revised 2021, 2023

Contents

IMPORTANT: Before making these recipes, please refer to the "Sweetener Conversion Guide" on page xxii. Sweetener options are available for special needs: such as allergies, a sensitive digestive system that cannot tolerate fiber or on medications that fiber can interfere with.

NOTE: If you are just beginning to add more fiber to your diet, and you want guidance on how to gradually increase it, refer to page xxiii. This guide is also helpful for those who want to convert the refined sweeteners to healthy low-glycemic sweeteners in their own favorite recipes. Also, you will notice throughout the book I included options with the recipes, so if you want, you can adjust it to your specific needs and taste.

With Gratitude

First of all, I want to thank the Lord for giving me the inspiration to write this book and to all those who have helped me through this journey.

I want to thank our physician for his scientific studies on how food affects the body. We are very grateful that we could benefit from his vast knowledge of information, especially about how our bodies are affected by the consumption of refined and processed foods. We are especially thankful to learn that high glycemic foods are a major contributor to inflammation in the body; therefore making healthier choices will help us to avoid many of the devastating disease processes that are so prevalent today. We are also thankful for our physician's desire to learn all there is to know about treating health. This book wouldn't be possible without him!

Also, I want to thank all my family and friends, who tested my recipes. A special thanks to my grandson, who said with a thumbs up, "these treats are grandson approved!" To his little brother that would always grab a chair to bake by my side. It's great to see my grandchildren's love for baking! Thank you to my daughter who believed in me and pushed me to pursue this dream and for her beautiful design ideas. Also, thank you to my son for creating and designing the website. And to my family and friends who supported me with prayers and encouragement. Most of all, I'm thankful for the support of my husband, who put up with my messy baking!

Next, I would like to thank my photographer, Melissa Alderton, www.melissaaldertonphotography.com, who did a fantastic job capturing the farm theme throughout all the pictures. All of the desserts, treats, beverages and sauces look beautiful! Some of the props were original from my mom's kitchen on the farm, which made the pictures that much more special. Also, thank you to graphic design artist, Sheryl Hildebrand-Marsh, for beginning the process with her initial design concepts.

Finally, thank you to my sister-in-law and nephew who invested their time to help with the proofreading and revision of this printed book and the e-book and also to my daughter-in-law who helped with the software setup. It's been a pleasure working with them.

My Personal Journey

My health journey began as a child. My mother, being 100% Swedish, loved her sweets! She was always baking wonderful desserts and treats. I also recall, during most of my childhood, my mother fought the "battle of the bulge" without lasting results. She finally gave up and just enjoyed all those delicious desserts and treats the rest of her life. Nothing wrong with that, but it may have had a damaging affect on her weight and health.

I grew up loving those desserts myself and always had an abundance of them available at all times. I became very addicted to sugar, and in addition, began a journey of developing many health problems. My immune system was weakened and I was often sick with colds and flus. Along with that, I struggled with allergies and asthma. Later in life, I developed hypoglycemia, bladder infections and chronic fatigue. I will never forget those years of weight gain and yoyo dieting.

Meanwhile, I knew my father had an interest in nutrition. Although he did not have the sweet tooth my mother and I did that contributed to our health problems, he wanted to prevent disease from happening. He lived a healthy and active life until passing just before his 98th birthday. He instilled in me the need for healthy eating. Therefore, I started eating better and cutting down on or eliminating the sweets. It was very hard to do and I didn't want to eliminate them, but I had no choice.

When I met my husband, he introduced me to food supplements. Food supplements helped to fill in those nutritional gaps I had in my diet. My health improved dramatically when I changed my diet and added food supplements. Now that I was married and had children, I didn't want them to grow up eating like I did as a child. Also, with bad genetics, my husband, his uncle, his parents and three brothers, all at a young age developed heart disease; I knew it was time to get serious. I had been invited to hear a doctor speak on "The Role of Nutrition in the Prevention of Cancer, Diabetes, & Heart Disease". What this doctor said made the most sense of anything I had learned so far, especially what I learned about the negative affects to our health from eating a diet of refined and processed foods, causing inflammation. I began developing my own recipes according to his research on the role nutrition plays in preventing disease. When I would tell people about my recipes, many would say, "you need to do a cookbook, and I will buy it!" SO, that is how this cookbook was birthed into existence. I began a journey of researching and testing to find the most beneficial sweeteners to create low-glycemic recipes that are delicious as well. Now I pray you will enjoy these yummy desserts along with the benefits of building good health.

HOW TO BEGIN AN EXCITING JOURNEY TO BETTER HEATLH

This cookbook makes favorite desserts and treats a healthy part of your diet. So many times we feel guilty when we eat our favorite treats or desserts. Our guilt is for a good reason, because so many of our foods contain an abundance of refined sugars. These sugars are not only in our desserts and treats, they are also hidden in our packaged foods, drinks and even the condiments we put on our food.

If you want your food to work for you and not against you, just start by taking a look at your diet:

>What is in your pantry?
>What type of foods do you crave?
>Do you read labels on the foods you purchase?

You will be surprised how much of the foods many of us consume are loaded with sugars and additives we don't need and won't miss when we get back to the basics of pure ingredients and whole foods. The problem really comes in when we add processed flour and sugars to our diet from breads and sweets. I know everyone enjoys these comfort foods and I am one of those people! Therefore, I decided I needed to figure out a way to have my cake and be healthy too! So I began by looking at all my favorite desserts and treats from my mom's recipe box and cookbooks. I loved all those wonderful desserts, but because of all the sugar they contained, I could no longer have them due to the fact I would get shortness of breath, even with just a taste. I had to finally give them up, until now!

I decided to remake all of my favorite recipes so they would not affect my health in a negative way. I was pleasantly surprised! When I would eat these desserts I was just waiting for something to happen, but it didn't! I knew I was on to something. I couldn't believe desserts and candies that tasted so good could be good for me!

To begin with, I needed to first look at my diet and the foods I purchased. I needed to see where I could make changes, but not sacrifice flavor. We all know if something doesn't suit our tastes, we won't eat or drink it. As I ate more natural foods, my taste began to change and all the processed foods I ate before did not taste as good as they once did. I realized I needed to use food in a way that builds up health, not tear it down.

I noticed for myself, if I eat a diet free from refined sugars, carbohydrates, and additives, along with the addition of food supplements, I maintain a steady weight, even without counting calories or consistent workouts. Since exercise is a vital part of good health, I know it is very important to make it a crucial part of my healthy routine.

For weight loss, keeping my blood sugar balanced is also an important component. By eating something approximately every 3 hours, I do not allow my blood sugar to drop. To help with this, an example of my meal plan would be: A small breakfast that consists of a protein shake with fruit or egg and sprouted grain toast, mid-morning snack; a piece of fruit, a light lunch; salad with protein, vegetables and fruit; afternoon snack; 1 or 2 tablespoons of nuts and raisins, a small dinner portion consisting of protein, vegetables/fruit, and before bed; a light snack of yogurt with fruit and natural sweeteners (no refined carbohydrates or sugars of course). For a treat, the "Chocolate Peanut Butter Melt-A-Ways" (on page 26) is what I reach for when I am on a weight loss plan. It contains a lot of protein, coconut oil and cocoa powder. Just one piece is rich in healthy nutrients and satisfies my sweet cravings without a lot of calories and carbohydrates. I eat smaller amounts of whole grain foods until I reach my goal.

For maintaining weight, I increase complex carbohydrates, such as my healthy desserts and more whole grains. Still, I want to continue portion control. Too much of anything, even healthy foods, isn't good and calories do add up, especially if you are not exercising regularly. A wonderful side benefit of my desserts is the addition of fiber, such as whole grains, fruits and the sugar substitute. Adding this fiber is critical, because it helps with balancing my blood sugar and regular elimination. It also helps me stay full and satisfied, therefore, great for maintaining my weight as well.

Recently diagnosed with autoimmune disease, it was necessary for me to make more changes to my diet. Needing to further reduce sugars, I developed another lower sugar option (see page xxiii, Option 3).

If bothered by grains, swapping out high carbohydrate flour with grain-free flour options may help as well. I personally have not tried it, but if you wish to avoid grains, you will need to research how to incorporate grain-free flour, such as almond flour, into your recipes since they do not perform the same as grain flour.

To help my digestion when adding more fiber to my diet, I take enzymes at the start of my meals and drink peppermint-ginger or fennel tea after my meals or snacks, if needed. I also realized that when adding more fiber to my diet, I will need to drink more water! Last but not least, I personally know stress affects my digestion. To avoid indigestion, I'm learning to relax, chew my food well and enjoy every bite!

To keep my digestive system healthy, I take prebiotics and probiotics on a regular basis. Research shows that prebiotics are what feed the probiotics (the good, friendly bacteria in the intestinal tract) and help them to multiply. It is shown that multiplying the good probiotics may help with digestion, build a strong immune system and keep inflammation at bay.

I prefer using "0" sugar fiber sweeteners because they are a prebiotic food. It's a sweetener with benefits! Chicory root fiber sweetener is a beneficial soluble prebiotic fiber.

As you can see, I like choices! Since I am someone who has special needs and can't eat all the same foods my family can, I wanted to develop recipes that give options. Starting with special needs for children, (shown on page 42); and as we grow older our needs change. Because of this, more options are available in the "Ingredient List and Replacements for Special Diets" & "Healthy Sweeteners" sections. So no matter what your diet restrictions are, you can enjoy recipes that will "Treat Your Health"!

DISCLAIMER: These statements are not meant to cure, treat or prevent any disease.

INGREDIENT LIST AND REPLACEMENTS FOR SPECIAL DIETS

BUTTERMILK REPLACEMENT: 1 cup of milk (dairy or non-dairy and 1 tablespoon of vinegar works great for replacing 1 cup of buttermilk in your recipes. Combine milk and vinegar in a small bowl or measuring cup. Let the milk sit at least 5 minutes to sour. Buttermilk, sour milk or yogurt will change the PH and improve rising in baked goods.

EGG REPLACEMENT: 1 tablespoon of ground flaxseed and 3 tablespoons of water works great for replacing an egg in your recipes. In a small bowl, add ground flaxseed to the water, stir and let sit for 5 minutes to form a gel. Add to baked goods.

Flaxseed egg replacement works better for making cookies. For cakes, I like to use a store brand egg replacer that will help it to rise. If not allergic, egg yolk can be added along with the flax or egg replacers to give your baked goods a richer flavor.

Tip: Whole flaxseed can be processed in a coffee grinder or food processor to make flaxseed meal. Grinding flaxseed when needed, can help retain more of its nutritional value, since the whole seed is kept intact until processing.

FLOUR AND THICKENERS:

ARROWROOT is similar to cornstarch. It is a fine, clear white powder used as a thickening agent in liquid based recipes. It is easily digestible and gluten free.

BARLEY FLOUR can replace some wheat flour in a recipe to add soluble fiber. Like oat flour, barley flour adds a tender, cake-like texture and is slightly sweet. For this reason, it is also good in dessert breads and sweet rolls. In yeast breads, you can substitute $\frac{1}{4}$ to $\frac{1}{3}$ of the wheat flour with barley flour. In quick breads, you can substitute $\frac{1}{2}$ of the wheat flour with barley flour.

EINKORN is the wheat of our ancestors, which has always been non-GMO. Einkorn flour can be used where a combination of white flour and whole grain flour is needed or can be used as a thickener in puddings, etc. If Einkorn flour is not available, replace it with organic white flour.

Note: As mentioned before, the only time I use white flour is in small amounts such as a thickener or when whole grain flour can be combined with it.

GLUTEN-FREE ALL-PURPOSE FLOUR can replace wheat flour if you are gluten intolerant. Choosing ones that contain garbanzo bean flour, fava bean flour and/or sorghum flour adds protein to the high carbohydrate content of brown rice, potato starch and tapioca flour, which is commonly used in gluten-free flour. Although; the flavor is a little milder in the ones using mostly rice flour. Choose what you prefer. If the dessert recipe is too moist, add ¼ cup more of the gluten-free flour or sorghum flour. *Note:* If the gluten-free flour you choose does not have a substance in it to replace the affects of gluten, you will need to add xanthan gum which duplicates gluten. Use ½ teaspoon per 1 cup of flour for quick breads and ¾ teaspoon per 1 cup of flour for yeast dough or up to 1 teaspoon xanthan gum per 1 cup of flour may be needed. Guar gum is good used in cold foods such as ice cream or pastry filling. Using citrus foods with a high acidic content, such as lemon juice, can cause guar gum to lose it's thickening abilities. You will want to use xanthan gum instead or increase guar gum. If gluten-free recipes become gummy, refer to "tip" instructions on page 11.

GRAHAM FLOUR is coarsely ground whole wheat flour. It contains all the germ, oil and fiber from whole wheat. It is used in rustic breads and classic graham crackers.

GRAIN-FREE FLOUR (ALMOND FLOUR) can replace grain flour, if you are sensitive to grains. If needing a strict grain-free diet, research for more information.

KAMUT has a nice taste and texture. It is higher in vitamins and minerals (especially zinc and magnesium) than traditional wheat. The protein content is also higher than in wheat. Kamut works well in baked goods, such as muffins, but will require more liquid.

OAT FLOUR can replace some of the wheat flour in these recipes because of its delicate and slightly sweet flavor. It has a cake-like texture and works well in sweet rolls and dessert breads. It is rich in B vitamins and soluble fiber. In yeast breads, you can substitute ¼ to ⅓ of the wheat flour with oat flour.

SORGHUM FLOUR is a high protein flour that is sometimes added to the gluten-free flour to boost the protein content; therefore, replacing or adding ¼ cup sorghum flour to dessert recipes will add extra protein.

SPELT is an ancient strain of wheat like kamut. Those with wheat allergies should first decide, with their doctor, if spelt flour would be a good substitute for wheat in theses recipes. According to the "Smart Bread Machine Recipes"; "Spelt makes an exceptional bread flour. It produces a high-rising loaf without the addition of gluten, but adding gluten may guarantee a higher rise. Spelt breads have a fine grain, soft texture, and slightly milder flavor than breads made from regular whole wheat flour. Spelt flour can replace regular whole wheat flour in any recipe; substitute 1 cup plus 1 tablespoon of spelt flour for 1 cup of whole wheat flour. When replacing refined wheat flour, substitute spelt one-for-one."

SPROUTED FLOUR Wheat or spelt can be used in place of regular whole wheat flour. Sprouted flour digests like a vegetable. It is much easier on my digestive system than non-sprouted flour.

WHOLE GRAIN FLOUR When replacing processed flour with whole grain flour, gluten will need to be added for bread to rise higher. Add 1½ teaspoons wheat gluten for each cup of whole wheat flour used. Add 2 to 3 teaspoons gluten per cup of other whole grain flour, like oat, barley and rye.

WHOLE WHEAT PASTRY FLOUR is used in the majority of these recipes to achieve a light texture in muffins, quick breads, pastries and pie crusts due to its low protein content. It is not recommended for yeast breads. Note: If whole wheat pastry flour is unavailable, it may be replaced per cup with ½ cup general purpose flour and ½ cup whole wheat flour.

NUTS & SEEDS add a nice crunch and flavor to many desserts and treats. They can be blended into nut butters and used to make wonderful tasting cookies and candies. They are rich in energy, protein, antioxidants, omega-3 fatty acids, vitamins and minerals. They also are an excellent source of monounsaturated-fatty acids.

ALMONDS, WALNUTS, HAZELNUTS & PEANUTS are all rich in vitamin E and B-Complex. Hazelnuts have the added benefit of being rich in dietary fiber. According to the "Nutrition and You" website, "peanuts contain an excellent source of resveratrol, a polyphenolic antioxidant. Recent research studies suggest that roasting/ boiling enhances antioxidant bio-availability in the peanuts."

To slow-roast nuts, preheat the oven to 300 degrees. On a baking pan, sprinkle nuts with oil (optional) and stir to coat. I like using the expeller-pressed peanut oil because it has a high smoke point and has a rich, nutty flavor (if you are allergic, you can use almond oil). Place the nuts in oven while it is preheating. This will ensure that the nuts will be tender (not tough) especially when roasting almonds. Bake for a total of 20 to 30 minutes (including the pre-heat time), stirring nuts after the first 10 to 15 minutes. Watch the nuts closely, so they do not burn. Remove them from the oven and let them cool. Salt the nuts, if desired. Store them in the refrigerator. *Note:* Softer nuts may finish roasting in half the time.

CHIA SEEDS are packed with healthy nutrients. Don't be fooled by their tiny size. Chia seeds contain large amounts of fiber, protein and the minerals calcium, manganese, magnesium and phosphorus. They also contain large amounts of omega-3 fatty acids and antioxidants. Almost all of the carbohydrates are in the fiber, which may help blood sugar. A study on type 2 diabetes showed lower blood pressure and lower inflammation markers when consuming chia seeds. They easily blend into smoothies, baked goods, yogurt, cereal, etc.

FLAX SEEDS are one of the top plant sources of omega-3 essential fatty acids. They also have beneficial dietary fiber (mucilage), which works as a binder and leavening agent in baked goods. Furthermore, flax seeds contain lignans, a class of phytoestrogens considered to have antioxidants.

SUNFLOWER SEEDS are especially rich in polyunsaturated fatty acids, called linoleic acids. They also are a good source of monounsaturated fatty acids, known as oleic acids. If peanut allergy, sunflower seed butter can replace peanut butter in "Monster Cookies". Sunflower seed butter can easily be made by blending seeds in food processor. Add enough neutral flavored oil after seeds are ground to make it creamy. Place in a glass jar and store in refrigerator. *Note:* If using avocado oil in sunflower seed butter, your cookies may turn green inside.

COLD OR EXPELLER-PRESSED: For healthier benefits, only select cold or expeller-pressed oils. Cold or expeller-pressed oils have a good level of antioxidants and a longer shelf life. According to "Sweet and Natural", "heat is particularly influential in oil production because each 10 degree increase in temperature dramatically raises the rate at which the fatty acids react with oxygen, potentially destroying nutrients and promoting spoilage, as well as creating carcinogens. Most mass market oils are obtained by solvent extraction, which involves the use of chemical solvents, some carcinogenic. These oils are also usually refined, a process during which temperatures can exceed 450 degrees."

COOKING OILS that have a high smoke point and a neutral flavor are the best choice for deep frying those healthy donuts. Look for oils that have a smoking point above 400 degrees.

COCONUT OIL: This oil has many beneficial qualities. For instance, it doesn't easily become rancid at room temperature or break down with high heat. It can be used to enhance baked goods and to fry foods at high temperatures safely. It may have health benefits as well. Coconut oil contains one of the healthiest fats, lauric acid. Research shows it may have anti-inflammatory properties and is gentle on the digestive system.

PEANUT OIL: If you are not allergic to peanuts, this is a very healthy oil that is low in saturated fats and has no cholesterol. According to the *"Nutrition and You"* website; "Peanut oil, being a vegetable oil, is a good source of plant sterols, especially B-sitosterol. It is one of the cooking oils with a high smoke point of 450 degrees."

ORGANIC ingredients are what I use most to avoid chemicals, such as pesticides, in food.

RAW APPLE CIDER VINEGAR & LEMON JUICE adds wonderful texture and taste to baked goods. Vinegar makes a great dough conditioner, by adding lightness and volume to yeast breads. Raw vinegar contains strands of protein, enzymes and friendly bacteria, which may be beneficial to health. Scientific research shows raw apple cider vinegar may help with the glucose response to carbohydrates. Lemons are especially high in vitamin C and folate. Lemons contain compounds called limonins, which may help reduce LDL cholesterol.

SPICES add a wonderful flavor and aroma to many baked goods. They may have many health benefits as well.

CINNAMON is probably the most popular and well-known of all the spices. Cinnamon has a powerful sweet smelling aroma when used in baked goods and hot beverages. It is an excellent source of minerals and vitamins, and is a very good source of flavonoid phenolic antioxidants.

CLOVES have a sweet fragrance and flavor. It is used in small amounts in baked goods due to its powerful flavor. It contains health benefiting essential oils and antioxidant properties.

COCOA is used in making chocolate and other sweet delicacies. According to the "Medicine Hunter" website, "Cocoa, The Health Miracle" ; "the polyphenols in cocoa are cardio-protective in two ways. They help to reduce the oxidation of low-density lipoproteins (LDL), or so-called bad cholesterol. Oxidation of LDL is considered a major factor in the promotion of coronary disease, most notably heart attack and stroke. Additionally, polyphenols inhibit blood platelets from clumping together. Another dimension of the benefits of cocoa and chocolate consumption concerns mood. Cocoa is rich in agents that may enhance the production of various feel-good chemicals in the brain, notably serotonin and dopamine. *Note :* To receive only the health benefits and not the negative effects of chocolate, purchase it, or make it, with low-glycemic natural sweeteners.

CARDAMOM is a very aromatic spice. It is used in a variety of beverages and soups. Cardamom is known for its digestive properties. It also is known to have antioxidant properties. It contains a good source of potassium, calcium and magnesium; as well as an excellent source of iron and manganese.

CORIANDER has a pleasant, slightly peppery spiciness that adds a nice flavor to the cola syrup recipe (see page 104). It also can be used as a flavoring agent in sweet breads and cakes. Coriander seeds possess many plant-derived chemical compounds that may have antioxidant properties. It is also rich in fiber, minerals, vitamin C and B-complex.

GINGER is used in baked goods, candies and drinks. It has a pungent flavor and a spicy peppery taste. It is a wonderful addition to baked goods and drinks. It contains health benefiting essential oils.

NUTMEG features a warm, sweet aromatic flavor. It is a nice compliment to pies, cakes, donuts and custard. It contains a good source of vitamins, minerals and many flavonoid antioxidants.

TURMERIC has a mild peppery taste. It is rich in antioxidants and fiber. Studies show it has possible anti-inflammatory properties. Turmeric adds a layer of flavor to drinks and smoothies

Helpful Tip: If you experience digestive issues from eating grains, beans, legumes, nuts or seeds; try using sprouted grains and flour in place of the traditional kind. Soaking and cooking grains, beans and legumes, along with a pinch of baking soda, may help ease digestion. Also, it may be helpful to soak nuts and seeds in salt water overnight, rinsing and drying them before eating or roasting. Using fermented foods, like raw apple cider vinegar, is a wonderful addition as well, by allowing beneficial bacteria to help with digestion. Research these food processes, if you desire more detailed information.

CHICORY ROOT FIBER is also a low-glycemic sweetener with added health benefits. Chicory root fiber is a beneficial soluble, prebiotic fiber that promotes digestive health, supports beneficial bacteria in the colon, and may lower insulin resistance. Since chicory root is an excellent source of natural dietary fiber, it may help in the management of weight and weight loss.

DATES add that extra richness and flavor to desserts. The recipe for "Date Paste" is on page 66. Dates contain a rich source of nutrients. They are known to be an excellent source of iron, potassium, flavonoid polyphenolic anti-oxidants, and dietary fiber.

DATE SUGAR is made from 100% ground dried dates. This pure, unrefined sugar is a fiber-rich superfood that is a great substitute for other sugars. It may also be gentler on the digestive tract than sugar alcohol or chicory root fiber sweetener. Note: Date sugar works great in baked goods but not in beverages since it does not dissolve well in liquids due to fiber content. Also, to achieve the desired level of sweetness in baked goods, add pure stevia or pure monk fruit, to taste (for example: when using 1 tablespoon date sugar in a recipe, add ⅛ teaspoon more pure stevia or ¼ teaspoon pure monk fruit).

HONEY/CREAMED is raw honey that has not been altered, it has not been heated, filtered or pasteurized; therefore, it maintains all the natural healthful benefits from the hive. It is solid at room temperature and has a creamy consistency. It is perfect for fillings and spreads.

HONEY/RAW is used in my no-bake treats or where low-temperature heat is used, to help preserve the beneficial properties of the raw honey. If raw honey hardens, it will scoop easily when measuring for recipes. Liquid honey is easier for blending into sauces and beverages. To liquefy hardened honey, place in pan, heat to warm (not hot).

Tip: Before measuring honey, coat the inside of the utensils with oil for easy removal. For more information on the benefits of raw honey, research the studies that have been done on the anti-microbial properties, anti-inflammatory and anti-oxidant activity.

CAUTION: Honey is not recommended for children under the age of one.

MAPLE SYRUP is used in all of my recipes where heat is applied at high temperatures. It has a medium glycemic index. For this reason, I needed to lower the quantity of maple syrup and add fiber rich ingredients to help bring down the glycemic index in these recipes. Research shows, maple syrup may have antioxidant and anti-inflammatory properties. To learn more about this research and the many beneficial compounds found in maple syrup, see the university studies.

MOLASSES is a by-product obtained from processing sugar cane and beet sugar into refined table sugar. Molasses is used in small amounts in the recipes to add a rich flavor. It is especially good when added to caramel corn, barbeque sauce and baked beans. Molasses has a glycemic index similar to maple syrup. Since only a small amount is used in the recipes, the glycemic index is low. Molasses is rich in anti-oxidants and trace minerals. It is also a good source of iron and chromium.

MONK FRUIT is also a safe, natural alternative to chemical sweeteners that are "0" or low-glycemic. Since it is 150 to 200 times sweeter than sugar, only ¼ teaspoon to ½ teaspoon is used to replace refined sugar in these recipes. Monk fruit can be used in place of stevia in these recipes, if preferred to stevia. Since it is about half as sweet as stevia, you would need to use twice the amount of monk fruit. Example: ¼ teaspoon monk fruit replaces ⅛ teaspoon stevia. Again, monk fruit, like stevia, is very concentrated and a little goes a long way. If used correctly, these sweeteners work great for enhancing the sweetness and flavors in desserts and treats. If too much is used, it may have an aftertaste. Just the right amount keeps everything in balance.

Note: Lo Han is another name for monk fruit. I use one that contains the prebiotic, inulin. Monk fruit can be purchased at local grocery and health food stores or on-line. Also note, whatever monk fruit you purchase can vary in strength of sweetness. If you buy one that lists a different sweetener as the main ingredient, you may have to adjust the amount in the recipe. They may not be the same sweetness as the one I used with inulin. The same goes for stevia. Not all stevia products are the same and some brands will require more to get the same amount of sweetness in these recipes. Stevia should be the first and main ingredient listed on the bottle.

STEVIA is a safe, natural alternative to chemical sweeteners that are "0" or low-glycemic. Stevia is a healthier choice due to the fact it is shown not to raise blood sugar levels. Since the goal is not to raise blood sugar level in the body, this is an excellent addition to our choice of sweeteners. Again, this is one that is used in small amounts. According to "Nature's Sweet Secret", "Stevia extract 85-95% is between 200-300 times sweeter than sugar." (This is the stevia extract I prefer to use). If you notice, most of my recipes only call for ⅛- ¼ teaspoon, hence, it aids in reducing the amount of sweeteners used in a recipe that calls for large amounts of sugar. I am able to cut down half or more of the honey and maple syrup in my recipes. This helps to keep recipes low-glycemic. Stevia is not affected by heat, having a high temperature tolerance. Being a non-carbohydrate sweetener,stevia does not favor the growth of certain bacteria in the mouth that contribute to tooth decay. Furthermore, research shows it may have natural antioxidants. Stevia is a safe, low calorie alternative, especially in carbohydrate restricted diets.

Pure stevia is 100% stevia without any fillers or additives; such as erythritol, xylitol, maltodextrin, dextrose, inulin, or glycerin. To achieve the desired sweetness in these recipes, pure stevia must be used. If a stevia blend is used, containing any of the fillers or additives mentioned above, it would take a larger amount of it to reach the sweetness level of the pure stevia used in these recipes. Pure stevia or organic pure stevia can be purchased at your local health store or on line. Depending on the brand of stevia, level of sweetness varies.

INGREDIENT NURITION DATA CALULATOR is helpful for those who have to be on a strict diet, due to having diabetes, heart disease or cancer. These calculators can be found on line.

SWEETENER CONVERSION GUIDE

When I began my research for converting recipes, I was shocked to find how much refined sugar is in desserts, sauces and salad dressings. Most recipes use 1 to 2 cups of white or powdered sugar. Some recipes even had up to 4 cups of powdered sugar!

I researched to find the best options that were not only low-glycemic, but healthy as well. I also needed to find natural sweeteners that would replace the bulk of the processed sugars in my recipes. I decided raw honey and maple syrup would work best. In my research, I found raw honey is low-glycemic. When kept in this raw state, honey retains all its nutrients and these properties do not change much at low-temperature, stove-top heating. Also, studies were showing raw honey was not affecting blood sugar, unlike processed, refined sugar. When I researched maple syrup it showed to be a medium-low glycemic sweetener. Studies are showing maple syrup has possible benefits for blood sugar levels as well.

Even though this all sounds good, high quantities of honey or maple syrup increases the glycemic index and calories in recipes. I began my search for "0" to low-glycemic sweeteners that I could add to help reduce the amount of honey and maple syrup in my recipes. I found chicory root fiber sweetener, which is a natural soluble prebiotic fiber sweetener, that has "0" grams of sugar. This beneficial fiber sweetener helps bring down the glycemic index even further. After some experimentation, I found by adding a pure stevia product, it enhanced the sweetness of the foods I was creating. Monk fruit was another powerful sweetener, where a little goes along way. It is another option, if you prefer it over stevia, measure for measure it is half as sweet. In some recipes, I use a combination of monk fruit and stevia.

Also, adding whole grains to the recipes help to further reduce the glycemic index value in comparison to refined flours. When changing from dry to liquid sweeteners, I found I did not need to increase the whole grain flour measurement because whole grain flour requires more liquid.

In conclusion, by replacing refined ingredients with fiber sweeteners and whole grain flour (along with the addition of proteins and fats), have all been shown to help slow down the release of sugar into the blood stream.

Option #1: If chicory root fiber sweetener is chosen as your sugar substitute in these recipes and you need to slowly add fiber to your diet; change 2 tablespoons of sugar substitute to 1 tablespoon and add ¼ teaspoon monk fruit. If a recipe says 1 tablespoon of sugar substitute change to ½ tablespoon and add ½ teaspoon monk fruit. Since this is trial and error, you may need to adjust to taste. If you are tolerating the fiber sweetener well and want to increase it, follow the original recipe.

Option#2: If fiber is not well tolerated and you would prefer to use a non-fiber sugar substitute, see bottom of page 126 for another option. Some sugar substitutes don't have the same intensity of sweetness and more may need to be added for desired taste. If another option is chosen and the same sugar substitute measurement in the recipe is used, may need to add ¼ to ½ teaspoon monk fruit to increase the level of sweetness desired.

Option #3: If chicory root fiber sweetener is chosen and you want to reduce sugar and fiber to amounts that are well tolerated, the maple syrup and fiber sweetener can be adjusted. For example; reduce maple syrup by one measurement from ½ cup to ⅓ cup and reduce fiber sweetener from 1-2 tablespoons to 1-2 teaspoons. When reducing these two sweeteners, you will need to add other sweeteners to reach the same level of sweetness in the recipes. For example, also add; 1tablespoon low-glycemic date sugar or a zero-fiber/zero sugar substitute of your choice. If more sweetness is needed, add ¼ teaspoon monk fruit. Again, since this is trial and error, recipe may need to be adjusted to taste.

No-bake: My formula for creating a low-glycemic dessert consists of a combination of the natural sweeteners. This formula has been consistent in the baked recipes, but not in the no-bake recipes. Since the formula for no-bake recipes is not consistent, converting each recipe is a matter of trial and error. The measurements are dependent upon the number and amount of ingredients in each recipe.

Caution: If anyone has health issues, allergies or on medications that fiber can interfere with, cannot tolerate high fiber foods or just have delicate digestive system, especially children and those eating fast food diets, may need to replace the fiber sweetener with other options, see page 126. Excessive consumption of chicory root fiber sweetener may cause digestive disturbances, especially if sugar is combined with it.

Note: See page 126 "Important Note about Fiber Sweeteners" for coconut sugar guidelines. If batter becomes too dry when replacing maple syrup with coconut sugar, may need to increase liquid. If using another sugar substitute or gluten-free flour and the batter becomes too wet, add a little more flour to get the right consistency. If adding more flour reduces the sweetness, add more sweetener of your choice, to taste.

SWEETENER CONVERSION EXAMPLES

Peanut Butter Rice Crispy Bars

Refined sugar: ½ c. corn syrup, ½ c. white sugar

Convert to low-glycemic sweeteners: ½ c. raw honey, sprinkle stevia or ¼ c. raw honey, ¼ c. brown rice syrup, ⅛ t. stevia

Caramels

Refined sugar: 1 c. corn syrup, 1 c. white sugar

Convert to low-glycemic sweeteners: ¼ c. maple syrup, ¼ c. raw honey, ½ to 1 T. sugar substitute, ½ t. stevia

Caramel Corn

Refined sugar: 1 c. brown sugar, ¼ c. corn syrup

Convert to low-glycemic sweeteners: ½ c. maple syrup, 1 T. molasses, ½ to 1 t. sugar substitute, ¼ t. monk fruit, ⅛ t. stevia

Cream Cheese Frosting

Refined sugar: 3 to 3½ c. powder sugar

Convert to low-glycemic sweeteners: 2 T. raw honey, 4 T. maple syrup, 1 t. sugar substitute, ¼ t. stevia

Creamy Chocolate Frosting

Refined sugar: 4 c. powder sugar

Convert to low-glycemic sweeteners: ⅓ c. maple syrup, ¼ c. raw honey, ½ to 1 T. sugar substitute, ¼ t. stevia

Homemade Vanilla Ice Cream
Refined sugar: 1 c. white sugar

Convert to low-glycemic sweeteners: ⅓ c. raw honey, 1 T. maple syrup, ⅛ to ¼ t. sugar substitute, ¼ t. stevia

Cheese Cake
Refined sugar: 1 c. white sugar

Convert to low-glycemic sweeteners: ½ c. maple syrup, 1 T. sugar substitute, ½ t. stevia

French Dressing
Refined sugar: ½ to 1 c. white sugar, ½ to ¾ c. ketchup

Convert to low-glycemic sweeteners; ⅓ c. Homemade Ketchup, ¼ c. maple syrup, ⅛ t. stevia

Cole Slaw Dressing
Refined sugar: ½ c. white sugar

Convert to low-glycemic sweeteners: 2 T. maple syrup, ⅛ t. stevia

Lemonade
Refined sugar: 1½ c. white sugar

Convert to low-glycemic sweeteners: ¼ c. raw honey, ¼ c. maple syrup, ½ t. stevia

Note: To see sugar substitutes, refer to page 126.

BREAKFAST

Fluffy Buttermilk Pancakes

Our family loves pancakes! These are a big hit with the grandkids. Light and fluffy, melt in your mouth, just the way we like 'em!

Makes 10 to 12 pancakes.

Set up electric griddle coated with unrefined cold-pressed coconut oil. Use more oil as needed while frying pancakes. Wait to heat griddle until pancake batter is made.

In a small bowl, combine milk and vinegar, let sit for at least 5 minutes to sour. In a medium bowl, combine flour, baking powder, baking soda, sugar substitute and salt. In a one quart mixing bowl with pour spout, whisk egg, oil and soured milk. Add the dry ingredients to all the wet ingredients. Batter will thicken as it sits. On heated griddle, pour batter to make pancakes 4 to 5 inches in diameter. Fry pancakes until puffed and a little dry around the edges. Turn and cook other side until golden brown.

Note: All dairy milk or non-dairy milk can be used, if desired. Also, all whole wheat pastry flour can be used. **

Option: Immediately after pouring batter on to griddle, sprinkle a few dark chocolate chips or blueberries on each pancake.

½ cup 2% or whole milk

½ cup unsweetened vanilla almond milk

1 tablespoon raw apple cider vinegar

½ cup whole wheat pastry flour

½ cup organic all-purpose flour **

1 teaspoon baking powder

½ teaspoon baking soda

½ teaspoon sugar substitute *

½ teaspoon salt

1 egg

1 tablespoon cold-pressed oil

*See page 126 for sugar substitute options.

Lemon Blueberry Muffins

When looking for a way to add more flavor to my mom's blueberry muffins, I immediately thought lemon would be a nice compliment to the blueberries. It was the perfect addition!

Serves 10 to 12.

Preheat oven to 350 degrees. Grease and lightly flour muffin pan or use paper liners. Make "Muffin or Pie Crumb Topping" (page 92) and set aside.

In a medium mixing bowl, blend flour, baking powder, baking soda, salt, sugar substitute and stevia. In a large mixing bowl, beat egg and blend in lemon juice, lemon zest, maple syrup, milk, oil and vanilla. Slowly fold dry ingredients into wet ingredients just until moistened (do not over stir). Using ¼ measuring cup, scoop out enough to fill each muffin cup. With point of table knife, poke 5 or 6 berries in each muffin. Add a little crumb topping on each muffin. Bake for 20-25 minutes.

1¾-2 cups whole wheat pastry flour
1 teaspoon baking powder
1 teaspoon baking soda
½ teaspoon salt
1 tablespoon sugar substitute*
⅛ teaspoon stevia
1 egg (beaten)
2 tablespoons lemon juice
1 tablespoon lemon zest
½ cup maple syrup
½ cup milk (your choice)
½ cup oil (your choice)
½ teaspoon vanilla
¾ cup blueberries

*See page 126 for sugar substitute options.

Carrot Muffins

I was able to create a tastier carrot muffin by changing the carrot shreds. I like the appearance of the coarsely shredded carrots, but I found that finely shredding half the carrots gave it more flavor and added moisture.

Serves 10 to 12.

Preheat oven to 350 degrees. Grease and lightly flour muffin pan or use paper liners. Optional: Make "Muffin or Pie Crumb Topping" and set aside.

In a medium mixing bowl, blend flour, baking powder, baking soda, sugar substitute, stevia, cinnamon, and salt. In a small bowl, combine milk and vinegar. Let milk sit for 5 minutes to sour. In a large mixing bowl, beat egg and blend in oil, maple syrup and soured milk. Stir in the carrots, raisins and walnuts. Slowly fold dry ingredients into wet ingredients just to moisten (do not over stir). Fill muffin pan with batter and bake for 25 minutes.

Note: These are moist and delicious without the crumb topping, but with the addition of crumb topping it adds a nice taste and texture. To make "Muffin or Pie Crumb Topping," see recipe, page 92.

1½-1¾ cups whole wheat pastry flour or
    sprouted wheat flour
1 teaspoon baking powder
¼-½ teaspoon baking soda**
1 tablespoon sugar substitute*
⅛ teaspoon stevia
1 teaspoon cinnamon
½ teaspoon salt
½ cup milk (your choice)
½ tablespoon raw apple cider vinegar
1 egg (beaten)
¼ cup oil (your choice)
½ cup maple syrup
1 cup shredded carrots (½ cup finely
    chopped, ½ cup coarsely chopped)
¼ cup raisins (optional)
¼ cup walnuts

**See page 126 for sugar substitute options.

** Can use ½ teaspoon baking soda, if needed for rising, when adding the maximum amount of flour.

Banana Bread

A family favorite! Our daughter loves leaving some chunks of banana in the dough when making her bread. A few bites of banana in each slice!

Serves 12.

Preheat oven to 350 degrees. Grease and lightly flour loaf pan, set aside.

In a medium mixing bowl, blend whole grain flour, baking powder, baking soda, cinnamon, sugar substitute, stevia, salt and walnuts. In a small bowl or measuring cup with pour spout, blend milk and vinegar. Let milk sit for 5 minutes to sour. In a large bowl, beat eggs; stir in maple syrup, oil, sour milk, vanilla and bananas. Add dry ingredients to wet ingredients and slowly fold in dry ingredients just until moistened. Do not over mix. Fill loaf pan and bake for 1 hour.

Note: Place a tin foil tent over loaf the last 15 minutes to prevent it from darkening too much. If you prefer not to use tin foil, parchment paper may be used instead.

2½ cups whole wheat pastry or sprouted flour
1 teaspoon baking powder
1 teaspoon baking soda
2 teaspoons cinnamon
1 tablespoon sugar substitute*
⅛ teaspoon stevia
½ teaspoon salt
½ cup walnuts
¼ cup milk (your choice)
1 teaspoon raw apple cider vinegar
2 eggs
½ cup maple syrup
½ cup oil (your choice)
1 teaspoon vanilla
4 large bananas (mashed)

**See page 126 for sugar substitute options.

Sour Cream Coffee Cake

A nice compliment to the morning cup of Joe! This also makes a great "Strawberry Shortcake" (see recipe, page 9).

Serves 12.

Preheat oven to 350 degrees. Grease and flour 2 quart baking dish or 9" pie pan. Make "Coffee Cake Crumb Topping" (page 9) and set aside.

In a medium bowl, blend the flour, sugar substitute, baking soda, baking powder, salt and stevia. In a large mixing bowl, blend the eggs, butter, maple syrup, sour cream and vanilla. Blend the dry ingredients into the wet ingredients until moistened. Do not over mix the batter. Add "Coffee Cake Crumb Topping" and bake for 25-30 minutes.

Tip: **If you like a dense coffee cake, cut the flour down to 1¾ cups.

Option: *Sweet, cinnamon, buttery center* - omit oatmeal and flour from "Coffee Cake Crumb Topping" and blend the remaining ingredients. Fill pan with half of the batter. Pour "sweet, cinnamon, buttery" mixture over batter. Pour the rest of the batter on top of this mixture. Last, add the original "Coffee Cake Crumb Topping" to give it a nice crunch!

2 cups whole pastry flour**
1 tablespoon sugar substitute*
1 teaspoon baking soda
½ teaspoon baking powder
½ teaspoon salt

⅛ teaspoon stevia
2 eggs
½ cup butter
⅔ cup maple syrup
1 cup sour cream
1 teaspoon vanilla

*See page 126 for sugar substitute options.

Coffee Cake Crumb Topping

Makes approximately 1 cup.

In a medium bowl, blend butter and maple syrup. In a small bowl, blend quick oats, flour, cinnamon, sugar substitute, salt and stevia. Add dry ingredients to wet ingredients. Mix in nuts. Sprinkle crumb mixture over top of batter before baking.

Note: **White flour makes the best crumble. If you prefer to use more whole grains, replace 2 tablespoons organic white flour with 2 tablespoons whole wheat pastry flour. If your preference is to use all whole wheat pastry flour, it will be more moist. You will need to chill crumble mixture until hardens just enough to break it apart to make crumbles.

2 tablespoons butter

2 tablespoons maple syrup

2 tablespoons dry quick oats

¼ cup organic white flour**

2 teaspoons cinnamon

½ teaspoon sugar substitute*

Pinch of salt, to taste

⅛ teaspoon stevia

½ cup nuts (optional)

*See page 126 for sugar substitute options.

Strawberry Shortcake

Serves 12.

To make "Strawberry Shortcake", follow "Sour Cream Coffee Cake" recipe on page 8. Omit "Coffee Cake Crumb Topping", pour batter into greased and floured pan. Bake for 25 minutes. Let cool. Serve shortcake with "Strawberry Topping" and "Whipped Cream Topping," page 93.

Strawberry Topping:
In small saucepan, mash fruit slightly to release the juices. Add maple syrup to taste, starting with 1 tablespoon. Add sugar substitute. If needed, add stevia to taste. Stir and simmer to desired consistency.

Option: To make a biscuit-style shortcake, refer to "Lemon Poppy Seed Scones" recipe on page 18. Grease and flour a 6" x 10" pan. If prefer to make individual biscuits, drop large scoops of dough on to cookie sheet. Since the dough is not rolled, it is not necessary to chill.

1½ cup strawberries (frozen or fresh)
1 tablespoon maple syrup
¼ teaspoon sugar substitute*
Sprinkle of stevia (optional)

*See page 126 for sugar substitute options.

Cinnamon Applesauce Muffins (Gluten-Free)

This is a wonderful moist and delicious muffin. I think everyone, including those who are not gluten sensitive, will enjoy it.

Serves 10 to 12.

Preheat oven to 350 degrees. Grease and lightly flour muffin pan or use paper liners.

In a medium bowl, mix flour, baking soda, baking powder, salt, cinnamon, sugar substitute and stevia. In a small bowl or measuring cup with pour spout, combine milk and vinegar. Let milk sit 5 minutes to sour. In a large bowl, beat egg and blend in maple syrup, oil, applesauce, soured milk and vanilla. Fold dry ingredients into wet ingredients. Do not over mix. Bake for 20-25 minutes. These muffins will become very moist in a warm environment and must be stored in the refrigerator.

Note: **If you only bake with gluten-free flour, you can replace any of the whole wheat pastry flour in these recipes with gluten-free flour as long as it has a similar texture to whole wheat pastry flour. If you chose a gluten-free flour blend that already has sorghum flour in it, just omit the sorghum flour and use 2 cups of the flour you have chosen. If muffins seem too moist, increase flour by 2 tablespoons to ¼ cup.

⅓ cup sorghum flour**

1⅔ cups gluten free all-purpose flour**

1 teaspoon baking soda

½ teaspoon baking powder

½ teaspoon salt

1-2 teaspoon cinnamon

¼ teaspoon nutmeg or allspice (optl.)

1 tablespoon sugar substitute*

⅛ teaspoon stevia

½ cup milk (your choice)

1 teaspoon raw apple cider vinegar

1 egg (beaten)

½ cup maple syrup

½ cup oil (your choice)

½ cup applesauce

1 teaspoon vanilla

*See page 126 for sugar substitute options.

Option: Add ½ cup diced apples or ¼ cup raisins and ½ cup walnuts.

Tip: If your muffins become gummy when using gluten-free rice flour blends, replace part of the 2 cups of flour with ¼ cup buckwheat or oat flour** (sometimes I like to combine the two flours, using 2 tablespoons of each to equal ¼ cup). **If you cannot find gluten-free oat flour, blend gluten-free oats or quick oats in a food processor until you reach the consistency of flour.

Caramel Pecan Rolls

These were a huge hit with my husband. He said they are the best caramel rolls ever! He wasn't sure if he could share them with anyone.

Serves 7 to 8.

Preheat oven to 350 degrees. Make caramel sauce just before dough is ready to put in 12" round pan.

To make dough:

In a small saucepan, heat the maple syrup and oil just until warm, not hot. Remove from heat, add yeast, stir and let sit 5 minutes to activate the yeast. In a small bowl, add milk and vinegar. Stir and let sit 5 minutes to sour milk. In microwave, warm the sour milk. Again, make sure it is not too hot. (Added instructions for dough #2 only: after souring milk, in a medium bowl, beat egg. Warm the milk, pumpkin and butter, blend with egg.) In bread machine, add all the wet ingredients. In a separate mixing bowl, blend flour and gluten. Add flour and gluten on top of wet ingredients. Add salt last. Set machine to dough cycle.

To make caramel sauce:

In a large saucepan or fry pan, combine all caramel sauce ingredients, except for nuts. On low heat, stir and simmer until bubbles appear, for about 10-15 minutes, or until caramel sauce slightly thickens, not hardens. Add nuts. Pour sauce and nuts into baking pan.

Caramel Sauce:

¼ cup butter

⅓ cup maple syrup

½ tablespoon sugar substitute*

Sprinkle of stevia

½ cup nuts

*See page 126 for sugar substitute options.

Dough #1:

2 tablespoons maple syrup

1 tablespoon oil (your choice)

1 teaspoon instant yeast

1 cup milk (your choice)

1 tablespoon raw apple cider vinegar

2 cups whole wheat sprouted flour**

1 tablespoon wheat gluten**

Sprinkle stevia (optional)

½ teaspoon salt

Filling:

⅛ cup butter

½-1 tablespoon cinnamon

Place dough on floured board and roll out dough to ½ inch thickness in the shape of a rectangle. On the entire surface of the dough, spread butter and sprinkle cinnamon. Starting on the wide side of the dough, roll dough into a cylinder shape and pinch edge to hold it together. Cut into 1 inch slices and lay rolls flat side down in the baking pan on top of caramel sauce and nuts. Cover and let rise in a warm place until doubled in size about 45 to 60 minutes. Bake for 15-20 minutes, or until lightly browned. Remove from oven and cool.

Note: **If gluten sensitive, replace wheat flour and gluten with organic sprouted or whole grain spelt flour. Spelt flour is an exceptional bread flour without the addition of gluten and is easier to digest. When omitting the gluten, add 1-2 tablespoons more spelt flour. Also refer to page xiv for instructions, when replacing wheat flour with spelt flour. If unable to tolerate spelt, look for gluten-free options when making bread or rolls.

Options: Dough #1 will make a light textured loaf of bread. Dough #2 will make light, fluffy and flavorful dinner rolls.

Dough #2:

2 tablespoons maple syrup

2 tablespoons water

1 teaspoon instant yeast

⅓ cup milk (your choice)

1 teaspoon raw apple cider vinegar

1 egg (beaten)

½ cup canned pumpkin

¼ cup butter

2¼ cups sprouted whole wheat flour**

1 tablespoon wheat gluten**

Sprinkle stevia, to taste

¾ teaspoon salt

Raised Donuts

Oh, how I remember as a little girl, going to the bakery and seeing all those freshly made raised donuts!I couldn't wait to enjoy every delicious bite! Such a guilty pleasure now made guilt-free! This sweet dough makes a very light and delicious donut.

Serves 12.

To make dough:

In a medium mixing bowl, combine flour, gluten, sugar subsitute, salt and stevia. In a large mixing bowl, dissolve yeast in warm water for about 5 minutes. To the yeast and water mixture, blend in potatoes, butter, maple syrup and beaten egg. Pour wet ingredients in to the bread machine. Place dry ingredients on top of wet ingredients in bread machine and start dough cycle. When cycle has finished, remove dough and place on a lightly floured surface. Roll out dough to ½ inch thick. Cut out donuts with donut cutter. Remove excess dough, roll out and continue cutting out donuts until all dough is used. Cover and let donuts rise until double, about 1 hour.

Dough:

3 cups sprouted wheat flour**
1 tablespoon gluten**
1 tablespoon sugar substitute*
½ teaspoon salt
⅛ teaspoon stevia
1 teaspoon instant yeast
⅔ cup warm water
½ cup mashed potatoes
⅓ cup butter (softened)
⅓ cup maple syrup
1 egg (beaten)

Cooking oil (for deep frying)

*See page 126 for sugar substitute options.

Sweet cinnamon mixture: (for coating)

2 tablespoons sugar substitute
2 tablespoons cinnamon

In a cast iron fry pan or deep fat fryer, filled with 2 to 3 inches of oil, heat to 375 degrees (use deep fry thermometer). You may need to lower heat if donuts brown too quickly. Using a wide spatula, slide donuts into hot oil. Turn donuts as they rise to surface of oil. Fry donuts until golden brown, approximately 1 minute on each side. Drain on paper towel. Dip donuts in sugar substitute and cinnamon mixture or let donuts cool slightly and frost with "Chocolate Cake Frosting" (page 63).

Note: **If gluten sensitive, replace sprouted whole wheat flour and gluten with organic sprouted or whole grain spelt flour. Also refer to page xiv for instructions, when replacing wheat flour with spelt flour. Spelt flour, without the addition of gluten, is an exceptional bread flour and is easier for digestion. If unable to tolerate spelt, look for gluten-free flour options when making bread or donuts.

Option: This dough also makes a sweet bun for a sandwich or a burger. If you prefer bread or buns with less sweetness, refer to recipes on page 12 and 13.

Buttermilk Cake Donuts

My mom always had cake donuts on hand to enjoy with that special cup of coffee. For all the coffee and donut lovers everywhere, I knew I needed to create a lower glycemic version of the original. I was pleasantly surprised how these donuts reminded me of those from my childhood.

Serves 10 to 12.

In a medium mixing bowl, combine flour, sugar substitute, baking powder, baking soda, nutmeg, stevia and salt. In a small bowl, stir vinegar into milk and let sit for 5 minutes to sour. In a large bowl, blend maple syrup, egg yolks, soured milk and butter. Add dry ingredients to wet ingredients just until blended. Do not over mix. Place dough in a medium bowl, cover and chill in the refrigerator for one hour. After dough is chilled, place dough on floured surface. Dust top of dough with flour. Roll the dough out to a ½ inch thickness. Using a donut cutter, cut out donuts and/or donut holes.

Using a cast iron frying pan, pour cooking oil to at least 1-2 inches in depth and heat approximately 200-300 degrees (use a deep-fry thermometer to regulate temperature). Place donuts and/or donut holes in oil, a few at a time. Fry until they rise to the top of the oil and both sides are golden.

2½-3 cups whole wheat pastry flour**
2 tablespoons sugar substitute*
1½ teaspoons baking powder
¼ teaspoon baking soda
⅛ teaspoon nutmeg
⅛ teaspoon stevia
½ teaspoon salt
1½ teaspoons raw apple cider vinegar
½ cup milk (your choice)
½ cup maple syrup
2 egg yolks
3 tablespoons melted cooled butter

Cooking oil (for deep frying)

*See page 126 for sugar substitute options.

Sweet Cinnamon Mixture: (for coating)
2 tablespoons cinnamon
2 tablespoons sugar substitute

Mix enough to dust donuts or roll donut holes in after frying.

Note: **The flour measurement may need to be adjusted depending on which sugar substitute you choose. Sugar substitutes with higher fiber content, may require 2½-2⅔ cups flour. Zero or low fiber sugar substitute may require 2¾-3 cups of flour in this recipe.

Chocolate Hazelnut Spread

Finally, a healthier version to a very popular nut butter spread!

Makes approximately 1 cup.

In a medium saucepan, on low heat, combine all ingredients. Blend until smooth. Store in a small glass jar in the refrigerator.

Tip: This makes a wonderful dip for sliced apples.

Options: *To make your own nut butter, preheat oven to 350 degrees. On baking pan, spread raw nuts in a single layer. Bake for 10 to 15 minutes until lightly brown. Remove from the oven and cool. If using hazelnuts, after roasting remove the skins. On a plate, roll nuts in a clean kitchen towel. Remove as many loose skins as you can and discard the skins. In a food processor, blend the nuts until it becomes nut butter. Scrape sides occasionally. Blend until creamy.

2 tablespoons hazelnut butter or nut butter
of your choice*

2 tablespoons maple syrup

2 tablespoons raw honey

1 tablespoon unsweetened nut milk (your choice)

¼ teaspoon vanilla

2 tablespoons chocolate chips

2 tablespoons cocoa powder

¼ teaspoon monk fruit**

¼ teaspoon salt

⅛ teaspoon stevia

**If you don't have monk fruit, use 1 teaspoon sugar substitute (page 126).

Lemon Poppy Seed Scones

These are luscious and lemony! They are good with or without poppy seeds.

Serves 10 to 12.

Preheat oven to 375 degrees. Grease 12" round baking pan.

In a medium bowl, combine flour, baking powder, baking soda, salt, poppy seeds, sugar substitute and stevia. In a small bowl, blend cream and vinegar. Let cream sit for 5 minutes to sour. In a large bowl, beat egg, maple syrup, lemon zest, lemon juice, and soured cream. Cut butter into dry ingredients with pastry blender or fork. Mix the dry ingredients into the wet ingredients until a ball of dough forms. Don't over mix or it will become tough. Place dough in refrigerator to chill for at least an hour. On greased cookie sheet, place dough covered with plastic wrap and roll out to ½ inch thickness. Remove plastic wrap. Cut in to 3" triangle. Brush with melted butter. Sprinkle with mixture of sugar substitute and lemon crystals. Bake in oven for 15-25 minutes. Let cool. Can be stored in the freezer.

Tip: For freshly baked taste, reheat scones in microwave a few seconds or place covered dish in 350 degree oven, 5 to 10 minutes. This also works great for freshening homemade bread and buns.

2¼- 2⅔ cups whole wheat pastry flour
1½ teaspoons baking powder
¼ teaspoon baking soda
¼ teaspoon salt
1 tablespoon poppy seeds (optional)
2 tablespoons sugar substitute *
⅛ teaspoon stevia
½ cup cream
1½ teaspoons of raw apple cider vinegar
1 egg (beaten)
½ cup maple syrup
1 tablespoon lemon zest
1 tablespoon lemon juice
½ cup cold butter, cut into chunks

*See page 126 for sugar substitute options.

For top of scone:
¼ cup melted butter
2 teaspoons of sugar substitute
2 packets of lemon juice crystals.

These juice crystals can be found in the juice aisle at your local grocery store.

BREAKFAST   19

Cinnamon Raisin Granola

Trying to find a granola with plenty of flavor without the added refined sugar was difficult, until now! This granola is great with milk or just as a snack right out of the jar.

Approximately 10 (½ cup) servings.

Preheat oven to 325 degrees. Use 11" x 17" pan.

In a small saucepan, on medium-high heat, blend the maple syrup, sugar substitute, butter, coconut oil, cinnamon, salt, stevia and vanilla until bubbles. Turn the heat down to low and simmer for approximately 5 minutes. Pour syrup mixture over nuts, coconut and rolled oats. Mix thoroughly to coat. Spread into pan. Bake granola 10 to 20 minutes, depending if you want it chewy or crunchy (stir granola half way through baking.) Add raisins after removing from oven and mix them in while granola is still warm. Cool and break granola into pieces before storing in container (glass canning jar, etc.)

Note: ** Add raisins after baking or they will become tough.

½ cup maple syrup

1 tablespoon sugar substitute*

2 tablespoons butter

2 tablespoons coconut oil

1 teaspoons cinnamon

¼ teaspoon salt

⅛ teaspoon stevia

1 teaspoon vanilla

1 cup chopped walnuts

1 cup unsweetened coconut

2 cups rolled oats

½ cup raisins**

*See page 126 for sugar substitute options.

CANDY TREATS

Chocolate Frozen Bananas

On those rainy days, this is a fun and easy treat to make with your children.

Frozen banana
"Chocolate Peanut Butter Melt-A-Ways" (page 26)
Nuts or coconut (optional)

Remove peel. Use a whole banana or cut into 2" chunks. Insert treat stick. Place the banana on a plate and freeze until hard. Melt "Chocolate Peanut Butter Melt-A-Ways". Quickly dip frozen banana into chocolate or drizzle unto banana, hold the banana by the stick until chocolate hardens. Eat immediately or place back in freezer for later.

Options: Place chopped peanuts, almonds or coconut in a bowl. First, dip frozen banana in the chocolate. Before chocolate hardens on the banana, roll or sprinkle nuts or coconut on chocolate covered banana. Hold banana by stick until chocolate hardens, eat immediately or place back into freezer for later.

Chocolate Peppermint Drops

Need a quick and easy treat? These chocolates can be made in minutes!

Serves approximately 6.

....

In a small saucepan on low heat, melt chocolate chips, sprinkle stevia and blend. Using a candy mold of your choice, pour small amount of melted chocolate in mold. Using the back of a small spoon, coat each mold. Place chocolate coated mold into freezer. In a small mixing bowl, blend the honey and peppermint oil (or white filling option). Take mold out of freezer and fill will honey mixture. Make sure to leave enough room on top of the filling for more chocolate. Pour melted chocolate over honey mixture to seal it. Place candy mold back into the freezer to harden the chocolates. Store in refrigerator or freezer, your preference.

Tip: If coconut oil and/or honey has hardened, place these ingredients in a small sauce pan on low heat and blend in remaining ingredients. If it becomes liquefied, place in freezer until consistency is like peanut butter. Place filling in chocolate mold (see instructions).

Note: *Use chocolate chips with a cacao content of 60% or more and unrefined sugar if possible.

Chocolate Coating:
½ cup dark chocolate chips*
⅛ teaspoon stevia

Honey Filling:
¼ cup creamed honey**
2-4 drops peppermint oil, to taste

Option: White Filling:
½ cup coconut oil
2 tablespoons raw honey
½ teaspoon peppermint extract***
⅛ teaspoon salt
⅛ teaspoon stevia

(Double "Chocolate Coating" recipe)

**See explanation for creamed honey on page xix.

***Since peppermint extract has less potency than the oil, more is needed, adjust to taste.

Chocolate Peanut Butter Melt-A-Ways

Our daughter came up with this great idea: to melt the "Chocolate Peanut Butter Melt-A-Ways" and use it for ice cream topping. It makes a great hard shell chocolate coating! Also, great for dipping "Chocolate Frozen Bananas" (page 24).

½ cup crunchy peanut butter*
⅓ cup coconut oil
2 tablespoons butter
¼ cup raw honey
½ teaspoon vanilla
½ cup cocoa powder
¼ teaspoon salt
¼ teaspoon stevia

Serves 24.

In a medium saucepan on low heat, blend peanut butter, coconut oil, butter, honey and vanilla. Using a whisk, blend in cocoa, salt and stevia. Pour into candy molds and freeze to harden. Release candies from molds and place in a zipper bag or container. Store in the freezer.

Note: These will soften quickly. Eat immediately from freezer. *Option: replace peanut butter with almond or cashew butter.

Homemade Chocolate Chips

Oops! I forgot to buy chocolate chips!
No worries, I can make my own.

Makes approximately half cup.

In a small saucepan, melt the unsweetened baking chocolate and coconut oil. Add maple syrup, sugar substitute, salt, vanilla, and stevia. Make a pastry bag by cutting the corner of a plastic sandwich bag. Fill bag with melted chocolate. By twisting bag, it pushes the chocolate to the open corner. Over a plate, squeeze bag until chocolate comes out to form small chocolate chips. Place plate in freezer until the chips harden. Store chocolate chips in a container in the refrigerator or freezer until using them in your favorite cookies and bars.

2 ounce unsweetened baking chocolate
1 teaspoon coconut oil
4 teaspoons maple syrup
4 teaspoons sugar substitute*
⅛ teaspoon salt
⅛ teaspoon vanilla
⅛ teaspoon stevia

*See page 126 for sugar substitute options.

Chocolate Almond Coconut Candies

If you loved chocolate coconut almond candy as a child; as an adult, you will appreciate the healthy ingredients along with the taste you remembered!

Serves 36.

In small saucepan, over low heat, melt honey. Stir in sweetened condensed milk, salt, vanilla and stevia. Simmer approximately 5 minutes, then add shredded coconut. Turn off heat but leave saucepan on burner, and blend well until a sticky ball forms. Chill in refrigerator. Combine the chocolate coating ingredients in a saucepan. Fill half of each candy mold with the melted chocolate. Place one small ball of coconut mixture into each mold. Place almond on top of coconut mixture and press down. Be sure to leave enough room for more chocolate coating. Place in freezer to harden and store.

Option: "Chocolate Coating for Peanut Butter Cups" (see recipe, page 31).

¼ cup raw honey

7 ounces "Homemade Sweetened
  Condensed Milk" (page 65)

⅛ teaspoon salt

1 teaspoon vanilla

⅛ teaspoon stevia

2 cups unsweetened coconut
  (finely ground)

½ cup whole toasted almonds (optional)

Chocolate Coating:

"Chocolate Peanut Butter Melt-A-Ways" (see recipe, page 26)

Chocolate Peanut Butter Cups

What is better than the combination of peanut butter and chocolate! Here is another guilt-free treat to add to your assortment of delicious and healthy chocolate candies.

Serves 8 to 12.

In a small bowl, mix peanut butter, maple syrup, raw honey, arrowroot, sugar substitute, salt and stevia. To make Chocolate Coating for Peanut Butter Cups, see recipe on page 31.

Option: For no fiber, replace sugar substitute with ¼ teaspoon monk fruit.

½ cup peanut butter
2 tablespoons maple syrup
2 tablespoons raw honey
1 teaspoon arrowroot
1 teaspoon sugar substitute*
¼ teaspoon salt
⅛ teaspoon stevia

*See page 126 for sugar substitute options.

Chocolate Coating for Peanut Butter Cups

Makes approximately half cup.

1 cup dark chocolate chips *
4 tablespoons butter
2 tablespoons raw honey
¼ teaspoon salt
⅛ teaspoon stevia

In a medium saucepan, melt chocolate chips, butter, raw honey, salt, and stevia. Using the back of a small spoon, coat each candy mold with melted chocolate. Place mold in the freezer for 5 minutes. Fill hardened chocolate with peanut butter filling. Cover filling with more melted chocolate to seal peanut butter candy. Place candy mold in freezer until chocolates are firm. Remove candy mold from freezer and release candies. Store container in the refrigerator. If freezing, thaw before eating.

Note: *Use chocolate chips with a cacao content of 60% or more and unrefined sugar if possible. When making "Chocolate Coating for Peanut Butter Cups", if using sugar-free chocolate chips that includes chicory root fiber sweetener, omit butter and honey and ONLY melt on LOW heat for coating to remain a creamy consistency.

Option: For another chocolate coating, see the recipe for "Chocolate Peanut Butter Melt-A-Ways" (page 26). Store in freezer only.

Chocolate Covered Cherries

Normally these candies are sooo sweet, a cavity develops just thinking about them! My mad scientist instincts kicked in to find the right combination of ingredients to make healthy, full-flavored, but not overly sweet, chocolate covered cherries! Oh what sweet success!

Serves approximately 12.

....

To marinate canned cherries: Place cherries and juice in a 8" x 8" glass pan. Add 2 to 3 tablespoons honey or maple syrup, 1 teaspoon vanilla, sprinkle stevia and a pinch of salt. Cover dish and chill in refrigerator for 24 to 48 hours. Drain the juice off the cherries and place cherries in dehydrator or in oven on low temperature. Dehydrate just enough to take out a little moisture. Make filling and coating.

Mix "almond cream filling" ingredients together until well blended. Using the back of a small spoon, coat candy molds with melted chocolate. Place chocolate coated mold in freezer. After the chocolate hardens, remove from freezer and fill chocolate mold with a drop of almond cream and a cherry. Cover the filling with melted chocolate to seal candies and freeze.

Note: *See explanation for creamed honey on page xix.

15 ounce cherries (in water or natural juice)
2 tablespoons maple syrup
1 teaspoon vanilla

⅛ teaspoon stevia
Pinch of salt

Almond Cream Filling:
¼ cup creamed honey*
1 tablespoon butter
½ teaspoon almond extract
Sprinkle of stevia (optional)

OR

¼ cup creamed honey*
¼ teaspoon almond extract
⅛ teaspoon salt
Sprinkle of stevia (optional)

Chocolate coating:
See "Chocolate Coating for Peanut Butter Cups" on page 31.

Caramel Corn

A perfect sweet and salty combination!

Serves approximately 12 to 16.

Preheat oven to 325 degrees. Use 9" x 13" cake pan.

Make popcorn, as per instructions. In a large bowl, add 16 cups of popped corn. In a medium saucepan, whisk to blend maple syrup, molasses, butter, sugar substitute, monk fruit and stevia. On medium-high, heat to a low boil. Turn down heat to medium-low and continue cooking until the mixture slightly thickens, approximately 8-10 minutes. Remove caramel syrup from heat, add baking soda and whisk until mixture turns foamy. Pour the syrup mixture over popcorn. Mix until popcorn is completely coated. Place the caramel corn in a 9" x 13" baking pan. Bake 10 minutes, stirring half way through baking time. Cool before storing in a bag or container.

Note: **If you don't have monk fruit, it can be omitted. If desire more sweetness after omitting monk fruit, increase stevia to ¼ teaspoon.

16 cups popped corn, salted
½ cup peanuts (optional)

Syrup:
½ cup maple syrup
1 tablespoon molasses
½ cup butter (softened)
1 teaspoon sugar substitute*
¼ teaspoon monk fruit**
⅛ teaspoon stevia

¼ teaspoon baking soda (add later)

*See page 126 for sugar substitute options.

Caramels

When nothing else will do, eating these buttery, sweet and salty morsels will satisfy those cravings! This is also wonderful as a caramel sauce for ice cream.

Serves 9 to 12.

....

Grease an 8" x 8" inch pan, set aside.

In a large stainless steel fry pan or pot, blend maple syrup, honey, sugar substitute, stevia, cream, butter and salt. If making caramel sauce, also add vanilla. If making caramel candies, add vanilla after mixture thickens. A candy thermometer can be used to monitor the temperature of the caramel mixture. This helps retain the nutrients in the honey when temperature is kept at 140 degrees or below. Set heat at medium-low to low. Watch temperature carefully. Add vanilla after 30-45 minutes. Stir occasionally until mixture forms a soft ball. Place in pan and cut into one inch squares. Cool and wrap in clear wrap or wax paper. Store in refrigerator.

Tip: To make caramel sauce for ice cream, reduce cooking time to reach a consistency that will easily pour. Also great for dipping sliced apples.

Option: Sprinkle plain caramels with sea salt, cover the caramel with chocolate coating or top the caramel with a pecan and then coat with chocolate. See the "Chocolate Coating for Peanut Butter Cups" on page 31.

¼ cup maple syrup

¼ cup raw honey

1 tablespoon sugar substitute*

¼-½ teaspoon stevia

1 cup cream

½ cup butter

½ teaspoon salt

1 teaspoon vanilla

*See page 126 for sugar substitute options.

Fruity Roll-Ups

If fruity roll-ups are a favorite snack at your house, Mom will appreciate this lower glycemic version without refined sugars or artificial colors!

Serves 10.

Preheat oven to 200 degrees. Use slotted broiler grate.

In a medium bowl, combine applesauce, pureed strawberries, maple syrup, sugar substitute, and stevia. Stir until well blended. May need to use a food processor for smoother consistency. Spread the mixture to an ⅛ inch thickness over parchment paper on a broiler grate. I prefer to use a flat pan with holes for ventilation. Dry fruit mixture in oven for approximately 4 hours. Dry until it becomes leathery, but not sticky. Let cool. Cut fruit leather into 1 inch strips and roll. Store in a glass container. And if it is hot weather, store in the refrigerator.

Note:　　If fruit mixture is spread too thin or dried too long, fruit leather will become brittle and break after baking. If areas of the fruit mixture are not drying as fast as others, use a large spoon or spatula to spread out thicker areas for fruit to dry evenly.

Option:　　If prefer, can replace sugar substitute with ½ teaspoon monk fruit.

1½ cups unsweetened applesauce
½ cup strawberries (pureed)
¼ cup maple syrup
1 teaspoon sugar substitute*
⅛ teaspoon stevia

*See page 126 for sugar substitute options.

See page 126 for sugar substitute options.

COOKIES AND BARS

Mint Chocolate Butter Cookies

Mint is always a favorite at Christmas time. Enjoy the perfect blend of mint and chocolate on a soft buttery cookie!

Makes 24 cookies.

Preheat oven to 350 degrees.

In a medium bowl, mix flour, sugar substitute, stevia, baking soda and salt. In a large bowl, blend butter, maple syrup, egg and vanilla. Add dry ingredients to wet ingredients and mix until well blended. Roll into one inch ball. Using thumb dipped in a little butter, oil or water, make a well for the chocolate center. If needed, redo well when cookie is warm, not hot. Do not add chocolate center until cookie is baked and cooled. Bake 8-10 minutes.

In a small saucepan, on low heat, melt the chocolate chips, butter, honey, salt and stevia. Remove chocolate mixture from heat and mix in peppermint oil. After the cookies cool, fill center of cookie with a small amount of the melted Chocolate Mint Icing.

Option: If prefer more sweetness in the butter cookie, add ¼ teaspoon monk fruit. To make a flavorful sugar cookie; reduce flour to 1½ cups, reduce salt to ¼ teaspoon and replace 1 whole egg with 1 egg yolk.

2 cups organic whole wheat pastry flour
1 tablespoon sugar substitute*
⅛ teaspoon stevia
½ teaspoon baking soda
½ teaspoon salt
½ cup butter
½ cup maple syrup
1 egg
1 teaspoon vanilla

*See page 126 for sugar substitute options.

Chocolate Mint Icing:
½ cup dark chocolate chips**
2 tablespoons butter
1 tablespoon raw honey
Pinch of salt
⅛ teaspoon stevia
2-4 drops peppermint oil, to taste

Note: **Use chocolate chip with a cacao content of 60% or more and unrefined sugar if possible. When making "Chocolate Mint Icing" if using sugar-free chocolate chips that includes the ingredient chicory root fiber sweetener, omit butter and honey and ONLY melt on LOW for icing to remain a creamy consistence.

Peanut Butter Cookies

These cookies are very soft and delicious. To top it off, add chocolate icing!

Makes 24 to 30 cookies.

Preheat oven to 350 degrees

In a medium bowl, mix flour, baking soda, sugar substitute, stevia and salt. In a large bowl, cream butter, peanut butter and blend in maple syrup, egg, and vanilla until smooth. Gradually add the dry ingredients to the wet ingredients. Chill dough. Roll into one inch balls. On a cookie sheet, using a fork, press down gently on each ball of dough, turn fork and press again, lightly, on cookie to make a criss-cross pattern. Bake 10-12 minutes. Let sit a couple of minutes before removing from hot cookie sheet. Let cookies cool completely on rack before lifting off.

Note: May need to dip fork into flour or melted butter occasionally between making criss-cross pattern to keep dough from sticking to the fork. If cookies become too moist, store in refrigerator or freezer. "Chocolate Icing", see page 42

2 cups plus 2 tablespoons whole wheat pastry flour
1 teaspoon baking soda
2 tablespoons sugar substitute*
⅛ teaspoon stevia
½ teaspoon salt
½ cup butter
½ cup organic unsweetened peanut butter
⅔ cup maple syrup
1 egg
1 teaspoon vanilla

*See page 126 for sugar substitute options.

Chocolate Icing for Peanut Butter Cookies

In a small saucepan, on low heat, combine chocolate chips, butter, raw honey, salt and stevia. After cookies cool, using a table knife, spread icing on top of cookies. Icing will harden as it cools.

½ cup dark chocolate chips*
2 tablespoons butter
1 tablespoon raw honey
Pinch of salt
⅛ teaspoon stevia

Note: *Use chocolate chips with a cacao content of 60% or more and unrefined sugar if possible. When making "Chocolate Icing for Peanut Butter Cookies", if using sugar-free chocolate chips that includes the ingredient chicory root fiber sweetener, omit butter and honey and ONLY melt on LOW for icing to remain a creamy consistence.

Important Note: Children and those who are eating a low fiber diet and/or processed food diet, may not tolerate 1-2 tablespoons fiber sweetener in these recipes. When replacing this sweetener with other options, refer to the "SUGAR SUBSTITUTES", page 126.

Chocolate Chip Cookies

Who doesn't like a warm chocolate chip cookie with a tall glass of cold milk!   This all-time favorite treat is now new and improved!

Makes 24 to 30 cookies.

Preheat oven to 350 degrees.

In a medium bowl, combine flour, baking soda, sugar substitute, stevia and salt. In a large bowl beat butter, maple syrup and vanilla. Add egg and beat well. Gradually blend dry ingredients into wet ingredients. Stir in the chocolate chips and the nuts. Chill in refrigerator for about an hour to firm dough. Drop by rounded tablespoon onto baking sheet. Bake for 10-12 minutes. Cookies are best eaten warm, right from the oven. These cookies will turn moist if left out. For best results, store in refrigerator or freezer. Reheat in toaster oven to restore freshly baked taste.

Tip: For a faster chill time, use a large spoon to spread the dough into a thin layer on a small cookie sheet or up the inside of the mixing bowl. Place in the freezer and chill for 10 to 15 minutes.

Note: **Use chocolate chips with a cacao content of 60% or more and unrefined sugar if possible.

2 cups whole wheat pastry flour

1 teaspoon baking soda

2 tablespoons sugar substitute*

⅛ teaspoon stevia

1 teaspoon salt

⅔ cup butter

⅔ cup maple syrup

1 teaspoon vanilla

1 egg

½ cup dark chocolate chips**

½ cup nuts

*See page 126 for sugar substitute options.

White Chocolate Chip Variation: Replace the dark chocolate chips with ½ cup sugar-free white chocolate chips and replace the nuts with ½ cup shredded coconut.

Gingerbread Cut-out Cookies

Making cut-out cookies is a fun activity during the holidays that brings the family together. We want to keep that beloved tradition going in a healthy way!

Makes 24 to 30 cookies.

Preheat oven to 350 degrees.

In a medium bowl, mix flour, sugar substitute, monk fruit, stevia, baking powder, baking soda, salt, cinnamon, ginger, cloves and nutmeg. In a large bowl, blend maple syrup, molasses and butter until smooth. Add egg and blend well. With a large spoon mix dry ingredients into wet ingredients until a soft dough forms. Chill for at least an hour or overnight to firm up dough. After chilling dough, roll out to ⅛ inch thick. With cookie cutters, cut dough into various shapes. Before baking, raisins and/or walnut pieces can be added for decoration. Bake 10-12 minutes. Store in refrigerator or freezer.

Tip: Can reduce spices in half if prefer a milder tasting cookie.

Note: **If dough seems too moist after final mix, can add 1 to 2 tablespoons of flour. If prefer more sweetness when adding flour, sprinkle a small amount of stevia or monk fruit.

Option: ***If you don't have monk fruit, increase stevia to ¼ teaspoon.

2⅓ cups whole wheat pastry flour**
2 tablespoons sugar substitute*
½ teaspoon monk fruit***
⅛ teaspoon stevia
1 teaspoon baking powder
½ teaspoon baking soda
½ teaspoon salt
1½-2 teaspoons cinnamon
1 teaspoon ginger
½ teaspoon cloves
½ teaspoon nutmeg
½ cup maple syrup
¼ cup molasses
½ cup butter (chilled)
1 egg

*See page 126 for sugar substitute options.

Decorative toppings:
Raisins
Walnut pieces
Ornamental Cookie Frosting recipe on page 68. (Frosting must be added after cookies are baked and completely cooled).

Oatmeal Raisin Cookies

This is one of my aunt's favorite recipes. I always loved the perfect balance of flavor and texture in this cookie! In memory of my aunt, I created the same yummy cookie without the refined sugars.

Makes 24 to 30 cookies.

Preheat oven to 350 degrees.

In a medium mixing bowl, combine the flour, quick oats, cinnamon, salt, sugar substitute, stevia and nuts. In a large mixing bowl, blend egg, butter, maple syrup, and vanilla. In a small glass or glass measuring cup, put in baking soda and set aside. In a medium saucepan, heat raisins and water. Simmer until raisins cook, just until water turns a light brown color. Pour 3 tablespoons of warm raisin juice into the baking soda and stir slightly to mix. When raisin juice is done fizzing, stir it into wet ingredients. Stir dry ingredients into wet ingredients until blended. Drop spoonfuls of batter onto cookie sheet. Bake 10 minutes until lightly browned.

1½ cups whole wheat pastry flour

¾ cup dry quick oats

½ teaspoon cinnamon

¼ teaspoon salt

1 tablespoon sugar substitute*

⅛ teaspoon stevia

⅓ cup walnuts

1 egg

½ cup butter

½ cup maple syrup

½ teaspoon vanilla

1 teaspoon baking soda

⅓ cup raisins

¼ cup water (reserve 3 tablespoons, refer to instructions)

*See page 126 for sugar substitute options.

Monster Cookies

These cookies are a big favorite at school bake sales and children's parties. Any cookie monster, I'm sure, would agree!

Makes approximately 36 cookies.

Preheat oven to 350 degrees. Grease a cookie sheet.

In a medium mixing bowl, combine oatmeal, baking soda, sugar substitute, stevia and salt. Place chocolate chips and chocolate drops on top of dry ingredients. In a large bowl, beat an egg, butter, peanut butter, maple syrup and vanilla. With a spoon, mix dry ingredients into wet ingredients. Place an egg sized amount of cookie dough on cookie sheet, press down slightly, space about two inches apart. Bake for approximately 10 minutes.

Tip: Since natural peanut butter separates from the oil, store an unopened jar upside-down. It will help absorb oil back into the peanut butter. When ready to use, turn jar over, open and gently stir. Store jar in refrigerator after opening.

Note: **Use chocolate chips with a cacao content of 60% or more and unrefined sugar if possible.

Option: If prefer a lower glycemic cookie, reduce maple syrup to ½ cup and increase sugar substitute to 2 tablespoons.

2¼ cups quick-cook oatmeal

1 teaspoon baking soda

1 tablespoon sugar substitute*

⅛ teaspoon stevia

¼ teaspoon salt

¼ cup dark chocolate chips**

¼ cup naturally colored, candy-coated chocolate drops

1 egg

¼ cup butter

1¼ cup organic unsweetened peanut butter

⅔ cup maple syrup

1 teaspoon vanilla

*See page 126 for sugar substitute options.

Fudge Brownies

After many, many attempts to create a fudgy, chewy brownie, without loading it with refined sugar, here it is!

Serves 8 to 12.

Preheat oven to 325 degrees. Grease and flour 6" x 10" pan.

In a medium bowl, blend flour, cocoa powder, sugar substitute, baking soda, stevia and salt In a large bowl, blend maple syrup, oil, egg yolks and vanilla. Stir in melted chocolate chips. Gently stir in dry ingredients. Pour into pan and bake for 20-30 minutes. Watch the baking time, so brownies do not dry out. Brownies may be done baking in 20 minutes.

Tip: When using gluten-free rice flour blends, to make it similar to the consistency of wheat flour, replace part of the gluten-free rice flour with 2 tablespoons of buckwheat flour, otherwise the batter may be too moist.

Note: **Use chocolate chips with a cacao content of 60% or more and unrefined sugar if possible.

⅔ cup whole wheat pastry flour

2 tablespoons cocoa powder

1 tablespoon sugar substitute*

⅛ teaspoon baking soda

⅛ teaspoon stevia

¼ teaspoon salt

⅔ cup maple syrup

½ cup oil (your choice)

2 egg yolks

½ teaspoon vanilla

¼ cup dark chocolate chips(melted)**

*See page 126 for sugar substitute options.

Coconut Date Ball

These coconut date ball are a wonderful snack when traveling or just when you need a quick pick-me-up.

Serves 10 to 12.

Lightly toast coconut and walnuts under broiler in oven. Watch carefully not to burn. Set aside to cool. In a medium saucepan combine maple syrup, honey, sugar substitute, egg, salt, chopped dates, date paste, cinnamon, vanilla and stevia. Heat ingredients on low heat until melted and blended well. Add toasted coconut and walnuts to this mixture. Continue to simmer on low heat while stirring until a sticky ball forms. While warm, form each into a one inch ball and roll in shredded coconut. Store in refrigerator or freezer.

Note: **If you are allergic to eggs, replace egg with a mixture of 1 tablespoon ground flaxseed and 2 tablespoons of water. Stir mixture and let sit to thicken. Once thickened combine with the rest of the ingredients.

Caution: Some pitted dates occasionally have pits, so always slice each date in half before processing to check for pits.

½ cup coconut (finely chopped)
1 cup walnuts (small pieces)
2 tablespoons maple syrup
2 tablespoons raw honey
1 teaspoon sugar substitute*
1 egg (beaten)**
¼ teaspoon salt
¼ cup dates (cut in small pieces)
½ cup "Date Paste" (page 66)
½ teaspoon cinnamon
¼ teaspoon vanilla

⅛ teaspoon stevia

Fine coconut (for rolling date ball)

*See page 126 for sugar substitute options.

Lemon Squares

Our neighbors enjoyed these lemon squares bursting with flavor and just the right amount of sweetness. A friend brought them to work. Her co-worker said she normally doesn't like lemon squares because they are overly sweet, but these she really liked!

Serves 18.

....

Preheat oven to 325 degrees. Grease and lightly flour a 6" x 10" pan.

To make the crust: In a small mixing bowl, blend the flour, sugar substitute, baking powder, salt and stevia. In a medium mixing bowl, blend the butter and maple syrup. Add the dry ingredients to the wet ingredients. Spread crust into pan.

To make the filling: In a small bowl, blend sugar substitute, arrowroot, stevia and salt. In a medium bowl, beat eggs; blend in maple syrup, lemon juice, and lemon zest. Add dry ingredients to wet ingredients. Blend and pour filling on top of crust.

Bake bars for 35-40 minutes.

Tip: Frozen whole lemons are easier to zest. Wear clean glove if lemons are too cold to handle while zesting.

Frosting: Cool squares and frost with "Ornamental Cookie Frosting" (see recipe on page 68). Store bars in the refrigerator or freezer. They will become too moist at room temperature.

Crust:

1 cup whole wheat pastry flour**

1 teaspoon sugar substitute

⅛ teaspoon baking powder

Pinch of salt

⅛ teaspoon stevia

½ cup butter

2 tablespoons maple syrup

Gluten-free crust: (Replace pastry flour)**

¾ cup plus 2 tablespoons gluten-free rice flour blend

1 tablespoon oat flour

1 tablespoon buckwheat flour

If too moist, reduce butter to ⅓ cup or add 2 to 3 tablespoons gluten-free flour.

Filling:

2 teaspoons sugar substitute*

1 tablespoon arrowroot

⅛ teaspoon stevia

⅛ teaspoon salt

2 eggs (beaten)

½ cup maple syrup

2 tablespoons lemon juice

1 tablespoon lemon zest

*See page 126 for sugar substitute options.

Pumpkin Bars

I remember my mom baking this wonderful autumn dessert. These pumpkin bars were a favorite at our house. Enjoy this healthier version to the original recipe!

Serves 32.

Preheat oven to 350 degrees. Grease and lightly flour a 12" x 15" bar pan.

In a medium bowl, mix flour, baking soda, baking powder, salt, cinnamon, ginger, nutmeg, sugar substitute and stevia. In a large bowl, beat eggs; blend in oil, maple syrup and pumpkin. Mix dry ingredients into wet ingredients until well blended. Pour into greased bar pan. Bake for 20 to 30 minutes. Watch carefully, bars may be done in 20 minutes.

Cool bars and frost with "Cream Cheese Frosting" recipe on page 68.

Note: If prefer more spice, add ⅛ teaspoon cloves.

Option: For a moist and flavorful pumpkin cake, reduce the maple syrup to ½ cup and add 2 tablespoons of "Date Paste" (page 66).

2½ cups organic whole wheat pastry flour
1 teaspoon baking soda
2 teaspoons baking powder
1 teaspoon salt
1-2 teaspoons cinnamon
½ teaspoon ginger
¼ teaspoon nutmeg
1 tablespoon sugar substitute *
⅛ teaspoon stevia
2 eggs
1 cup oil (your choice)
⅔ cup maple syrup
2 cups canned pumpkin (plain)

*See page 126 for sugar substitute options.

Peanut Butter Rice Crispy Bar or Ball

My kids grew up on these! These are a healthier alternative to the usual peanut butter rice crispy bars that are loaded with sugar. Your kids won't miss the sugar!

Serves 8 to 12.

In a medium mixing bowl, add rice crispy cereal. In a large mixing bowl, combine honey, peanut butter, butter, vanilla, cinnamon, salt and stevia. Mix rice crispy cereal into wet ingredients. Flatten rice crispy mixture into a greased 8" x 12" pan. Frost the bars with "Chocolate Icing for Peanut Butter Cookies" (page 42) Cut into 2 inch squares. Store bars in refrigerator.

Note: * Brown rice syrup adds a nice caramel-like flavor & sticky consistency. If you do not have brown rice syrup, it can be replaced with all raw honey.

Option: Roll each square into a ball. Make the chocolate icing and before it hardens, dip ball into melted chocolate to make a chocolate peanut butter ball. May need to double recipe for "Chocolate Icing".

3 cups organic brown rice crispy cereal
1/4 cup raw honey
1/4 cup brown rice syrup *
1/2 cup peanut butter
1 tablespoon butter
1/2 teaspoon vanilla
1/2 teaspoon cinnamon
Pinch of salt
Sprinkle of stevia (optional)

No Bake Energy Bars

Thanks to my neighbor for this delicious energy bar recipe! It is now the same delicious bar with a lower glycemic index.

Serves 8 to 12.

....

Grease a 6" x 12" pan.

In a medium mixing bowl, combine oatmeal, almond flour, flaxseed meal, cocoa powder, stevia, sunflower seeds and walnuts. In a large bowl, mix peanut butter, butter, coconut oil, melted chocolate chips and honey. Mix dry ingredients into wet ingredients. Press mixture into pan. These bars will soften quickly and best to eat immediately from freezer.

¼ cup oatmeal

¼ cup almond flour

¼ cup flaxseed meal

¼ cup cocoa powder

⅛ teaspoon stevia

¼ cup sunflower seeds

½ cup walnuts

½ cup peanut butter

2 tablespoons butter

2 tablespoons coconut oil

½ cup dark chocolate chips (melted)*

¼ cup raw honey

⅛ teaspoon salt**

Note: *Use chocolate chips with a cacao content of 60% or more and unrefined sugar if possible.

Option: **Lightly sprinkle salt over top of bars.

No Bake Chocolate Coconut Oat Drops (Haystacks)

Memories of haystacks on the farm!

Serves approximately 24.

In a large mixing bowl, add dry quick oats and coconut. In a medium mixing bowl, blend stevia, cocoa powder, and salt. In a medium saucepan, on low heat, blend honey, butter, coconut oil, peanut butter, and milk. Remove from heat and stir in vanilla. Add the stevia, cocoa powder, salt to wet mixture. Blend until smooth. Pour mixture over dry oats and coconut, stir until coated. Place spoonfuls of mixture onto a cookie sheet and place in refrigerator or freezer until cooled and hardened. Store candies in refrigerator or freezer.

Tip: *Replace ½ cup quick oats with ½ cup rolled oats.

Note: Increase stevia if more sweetness is desired.

3 cups dry quick oats *
½ cup coconut (fine)
⅛ teaspoon stevia
¼ cup cocoa powder
¼ teaspoon salt
⅓ cup raw honey
¼ cup butter
¼ cup coconut oil
½ cup peanut butter
¼ cup milk (your choice)
1 teaspoon vanilla

No Bake Coconut Cocoa Ball

These are so easy to make! A great treat to satisfy the sweet tooth and is healthy too!

Serves 8 to 12.

In a small saucepan, on low heat, warm honey, coconut oil. Blend in almond flour, cocoa powder, salt, stevia and vanilla. Add the coconut and walnuts. Stir until blended. Chill in refrigerator or freezer until firm. Remove from freezer and roll into 1 inch balls. Roll in coconut. Store candies in freezer.

¼ cup raw honey

¼ cup coconut oil

¼-⅓ cup almond flour

¼ cup cocoa powder

⅛ teaspoon salt

⅛ teaspoon stevia

1 teaspoon vanilla

½ cup finely shredded coconut (or less)

¼ cup chopped walnuts

Extra fine shredded coconut for coating

Six, Seven, or Eight Layer Bars!

Have a specific taste? This bar is for you! Choose your favorite toppings!

Serves 8 to 12.

Preheat oven to 350 degrees. Grease and lightly flour a 6" x 10" baking pan.

In the pan, stir melted butter and graham cracker crumbs. Using the bottom of a glass or measuring cup, press graham cracker crumbs evenly in the bottom of the pan. Over graham cracker crust, pour sweetened condensed milk to cover evenly. First sprinkle coconut, then nuts and chocolate chips. Bake for 25-35 minutes. When cooled, drizzle chocolate and/or caramel sauce on top, if desired. Chill in refrigerator before cutting bars into 1½ inch squares. Use a thin metal turner to remove bars easily. Store bars in refrigerator or freezer.

Tip: If some bars crumble, roll crumbles into a one inch ball and cover with finely shredded coconut.

Note: *Use chocolate chips with a cacao content of 60% or more and unrefined sugar if possible.

Crust:
⅓ cup butter, melted
1 cup "Homemade Graham Cracker
    Crumbs" (page 74)

Toppings:
1 cup (8 oz.) "Homemade Sweetened
    Condensed Milk" (page 65)
½ cup coconut (fine shreds work best)
½ cup nuts
¼ cup dark chocolate chips*

"Creamy Chocolate Frosting", optional
    (see recipe, page 63)

"Caramels" sauce, optional (see recipe,
page 34)

CAKES AND
ICE CREAM

Chocolate Cake or Cupcakes

When it comes to chocolate cake, I like a moist, fudgy cake. After many, many, many tries, I finally came up with the perfect combination that gave me the moist and flavorful cake I was looking for.

Serves 12 to 16.

Preheat oven to 325 degrees.

Grease and flour a 9" x 13" cake pan or cupcake pan lined with paper cups.

In a medium bowl, combine flour, baking soda, salt, sugar substitute and stevia. In a small bowl or measuring cup with pour spout, combine milk and vinegar. Let sit 5 minutes to sour. In a small saucepan, on low heat, melt chocolate squares. After chocolate is melted, blend in maple syrup. In a large mixing bowl, beat eggs; blend in sour milk, melted chocolate maple syrup mixture, date paste, oil, applesauce, and vanilla. Add dry ingredients to wet ingredients and blend until smooth. Bake for 20-30 minutes.

2 cups whole wheat pastry flour

1 teaspoon baking soda

1 teaspoon salt

2 tablespoons sugar substitute*

¼-½ teaspoon stevia

½ cup milk (your choice)

2 teaspoons apple cider vinegar

3 squares of unsweetened baking chocolate (melted)

⅔ cup maple syrup

2 eggs

½ cup "Date Paste" (page 66)

½ cup oil (your choice)

⅔ cup unsweetened applesauce

1 teaspoon vanilla

*See page 126 for sugar substitute options.

Creamy Chocolate Frosting

Makes approximately 1 cup.

In a saucepan, on low heat, melt chocolate chips. Add in remaining ingredients and blend. Cool frosting slightly, but not completely, so it easily spreads on cooled "Chocolate Cake or Cupcakes".

Note: **Use chocolate chips, with a cacao content of 60% or more and unrefined sugar, if possible. Sugar-free chocolate chips that include chicory root fiber sweetener may not work in this recipe. Low sugar chocolate chips may be the best option to maintain the creamy texture.

¾ cup dark chocolate chips**

¼ cup butter

¼ cup raw honey

⅓ cup maple syrup

½ teaspoon vanilla

1 tablespoon cocoa powder

1 tablespoon sugar substitute*

¼ teaspoon salt

⅛ teaspoon stevia

*See page 126 for sugar substitute options.

German Chocolate Frosting

Makes approximately 1 cup.

In a medium saucepan, whisk sweetened condensed milk, egg yolks and maple syrup until well blended. Add in sugar substitute, stevia, butter, vanilla and salt. Stir and cook on medium heat for 5 minutes. Add coconut and pecans. Continue to simmer on medium-low heat until it thickens (approximately 10 minutes). Remove from heat, stir in honey. Cool frosting slightly and spread on cooled "Chocolate Cake or Cupcakes", (page 62).

6-8 oz. "Homemade Sweetened
    Condensed Milk" (page 65)
2 egg yolks
2 tablespoons maple syrup
1 teaspoon sugar substitute*

⅛ teaspoon stevia
3 tablespoons butter
½ teaspoon vanilla
⅛ teaspoon salt
1 cup shredded coconut
½ cup chopped pecans
2 tablespoons raw honey

*See page 126 for sugar substitute options.

Homemade Sweetened Condensed Milk

Canned ready-made sweetened condensed milk is loaded with sugar. So it was a necessity for me to make this low-glycemic version!

Makes approximately 1 cup.

In medium saucepan, combine first 7 ingredients. Simmer for approximately 30 minutes. Add vanilla after milk is slightly thickened. If you cook it too long it will become rubbery. If it does become too thick, add more milk to thin it down; or if more sweetness is needed, add maple syrup instead. You should be able to pour it when finished cooking. It makes 6-8 oz. depending on how long it simmers. Let cool. Store in refrigerator until needed for recipes. It will thicken when chilled.

Tip: Using a wide bottom pot or pan will help the sweetened milk to thicken faster.

1 cup whole milk

2 tablespoons butter

4 tablespoons maple syrup

1 teaspoon arrowroot

1 teaspoon sugar substitute*

⅛ teaspoon stevia

⅛ teaspoon salt

¼ teaspoon vanilla

*See page 126 for sugar substitute options.

Date Paste

Makes approximately 1 cup.

1 cup dates
½ cup water

On a cutting board, cut each date in half to check for any pits. Chop dates into small pieces. In a small saucepan, on medium to medium-low heat, add water and dates. Simmer until dates are softened. Let cool and place softened dates and remaining water in food processor. Process dates until forms into a paste. Using spatula, scrape sides of container while processing. For leftover paste, place in a glass jar and freeze. It will still be soft enough to scoop out, while being stored in the freezer.

Note: To keep dates from sticking to side of container while processing and to achieve a smooth consistency, add small amounts of water while blending.

Carrot Cake

This is my favorite birthday cake! Great for that special day!

Serves 12 to 16.

Preheat oven to 350 degrees. Grease and lightly flour 13" x 9" cake pan.

In a medium mixing bowl blend together, flour, baking soda, baking powder, cinnamon, salt, stevia and sugar substitute. In a large mixing bowl, beat eggs; blend in maple syrup, date paste and oil. Mix in grated carrots. Fold dry ingredients into wet ingredients just until well mixed. Bake cake for 45 minutes (check at 30 minutes). Cool cake and frost with "Cream Cheese Frosting" (page 68) and top with walnuts (optional).

2 cups whole wheat pastry flour

2 teaspoons baking soda

½ teaspoon baking powder

2 teaspoons cinnamon

1 teaspoon salt

¼-½ teaspoon stevia

1 tablespoon sugar substitute*

4 eggs

⅔ cup maple syrup

¼ cup "Date Paste" (page 66)

1 cup oil (your choice)

3½ cups carrots (3 cups coarsely grated, ½ cup finely grated)

*See page 126 for sugar substitute options.

Cream Cheese Frosting

This is the perfect topping for carrot cake, without being overly sweet.

Makes approximately 1½ cups.

To make cream frosting
In small to medium mixing bowl, blend all ingredients with mixer until smooth. Spread on cooled "Carrot Cake" or "Pumpkin Bars".

To make ornamental cookie frosting
In small mixing bowl, blend all ingredients until smooth. In a pastry bag with a fine decorator tip, spoon frosting into bag. Decorate as desired.

Tip: Make a pastry bag by cutting the corner of a plasticsandwich bag. Fill bag with frosting. Twist top of bag to push frosting to open corner.

8 ounces cream cheese
¼ cup butter
2 tablespoons raw honey
¼ cup maple syrup
½ teaspoon vanilla
1 teaspoon sugar substitute *
⅛ teaspoon stevia
⅛ teaspoon salt

* See page 126 for sugar substitute options.

Ornamental Frosting
8 ounces cream cheese
2 tablespoons butter
2 tablespoons raw honey

⅛ teaspoon vanilla
¼ teaspoon monk fruit
1½ tablespoons arrowroot
⅛ teaspoon stevia
⅛ teaspoon salt

Homemade Vanilla Ice Cream

Since ice cream is one of my favorite desserts, it had to be one of my first creations. We love eating it homemade, right from the ice cream maker!

Makes approximately 1½ quarts.

In a large bowl, beat egg yolks; whisk in honey and maple syrup. Add cream, milk, sugar substitute, salt, stevia. Make double boiler (see "tip" below). Pour mixture into top fry pan, set temperature at medium-high or medium. Using candy thermometer, heat to temperature of 140 degrees. Reduce heat if necessary to maintain temperature. Stir mixture with whisk occasionally, while simmering until thickened to a consistency of watery pudding, or hey, melted ice cream! Take fry pan, containing pudding mixture, off of water-filled saute pan. Blend vanilla into pudding mixture. Pour into 2 quart casserole dish, cover and place in refrigerator over night to chill. If mixture is warm when placed in refrigerator, turn cover slightly to release excess moisture. Next day, pour mixture into ice cream maker.

Tip: To make a wide, low-sided double boiler, place a 12"stainless steel saute pan on the stove, then fill with water approximately 1½ to 2 inches from top of pan. Place a 12" stainless steel fry pan on top of saute pan.

Note: To add creamy texture to dairy-free ice cream, after mixture is warm, add in ¼ teaspoon of xanthan gum.

4 egg yolks

¼ cup raw honey

3-4 tablespoons maple syrup

2 cups cream

1 cup milk (dairy, lactose-free or non-dairy)

1 teaspoon sugar substitute*

¼ teaspoon salt

¼ teaspoon stevia

1 teaspoon vanilla

*See page 126 for sugar substitute options.

Cinnamon Maple Glazed Nuts

Want to add flavor and crunch to your freshly made vanilla ice cream? Try this flavorful topping. Also makes a great snack; easy to grab and go!

Makes 2 cups.

Preheat oven to 325 degrees.

In small saucepan, blend maple syrup, cinnamon, butter, fiber sweetener, salt, and vanilla. If need to pop the flavor, add a dusting of stevia. Place nuts in a medium baking dish. Pour syrup mixture over the nuts and stir until well coated.

Bake for 10-15 minutes. Cool before storing.

Note: To slow-roast nuts, refer to "Ingredient List" under the "Nuts & Seeds" section on page xv.

¼ cup maple syrup

1 teaspoon cinnamon

2 tablespoons butter

¼ teaspoon sugar substitute*

½ teaspoon salt

1 teaspoon vanilla

Light sprinkle of stevia (optional)

2 cups nuts

*See page 126 for sugar substitute options.

Chocolate Ice Cream Topping

This topping is similar to canned chocolate sauce. It is a thinner consistency for easier blending into ice cream or for a healthier version of chocolate milk!

Makes approximately 1 cup.

¼ cup water
⅓ cup raw honey
1 teaspoon vanilla
½ cup cocoa powder
⅛ teaspoon stevia
Pinch of salt

In a small saucepan, on low heat, blend water, honey and vanilla just until warm. Add cocoa powder, stevia and salt. Whisk until well blended. Store in refrigerator.

Homemade Graham Crackers

Makes 24 to 30 squares or 3 cups crumbs.

Preheat oven to 325 degrees.

In a medium bowl, blend flour, baking soda, salt, sugar substitute, and stevia. In a large bowl, blend molasses, maple syrup, butter and vanilla. Mix dry ingredients into wet ingredients until it forms a soft ball of dough. Cover with plastic wrap and chill for 30-60 minutes. Place dough on baking pan, place plastic wrap or parchment paper on top, press dough down on pan. Roll out dough to ⅛ inch (the thinner the cracker, the crispier it will be). Take off the parchment paper and cut into 2 inch squares with a pizza cutter. Poke holes in dough with a fork. Bake the graham crackers for 15 minutes. Let cool before storing in container.

Tip: Leave container open until dry to desired crispness.

¾ cup organic white flour
¾ cup whole wheat graham flour
½ teaspoon baking soda
¼ teaspoon salt
1 teaspoon sugar substitute*
¼-½ teaspoon stevia
1 teaspoon unsulphered molasses
⅓ cup maple syrup
½ cup butter or natural butter spread
¼ teaspoon vanilla

*See page 126 for sugar substitute options.

Graham Cracker Crust

Makes 1 crust.

Preheat oven to 350 degrees.

Blend together all ingredients and form into pie pan. For a pre-baked crust, bake for 8-10 minutes.

Tip: * To make crumbs, place graham crackers in a food processor or zipper bag and crush with rolling pin.

Note: Do not pre-bake crust for baked "Cheese Cake", page 76.

1½ cups "Homemade Graham Cracker Crumbs" (page 74) *
5 tablespoons butter (melted)

Cheese Cake

Ahhh! Always room for cheese cake!

Full recipe serves 12.

Preheat oven to 325 degrees.

Prepare the unbaked "Graham Cracker Crust" (see recipe, page 75). Press graham cracker crust into the bottom of a 10" x 10" cheese cake pan or glass baking dish. Using a food processor, blend cream cheese and sour cream until smooth. Add maple syrup, blend well. Add one egg at a time, pulse each time to blend. Finally add flour or arrowroot, stevia, monk fruit, sugar substitute, salt and vanilla. Blend well, scraping occasionally. Pour into unbaked graham cracker crust. Place a pan, half full of warm water, on bottom rack of oven (below the rack the cheese cake is on) or set the cheese cake in the pan of water, (called a water bath). Water should come up the outside of the pan to the level of the cheese cake batter. Bake cheese cake for 30 minutes. Turn off oven, keep oven door closed, and leave cheese cake in oven 30 minutes more. Remove from oven to cool on rack. Cover and refrigerate.

"Strawberry Topping", see "Strawberry Shortcake" recipe on bottom of page 9.

2 (8 ounce) packages regular cream cheese, cut into chunks
¼ cup sour cream
¾ cup maple syrup
3 eggs
1 tablespoon flour or arrowroot
⅛ teaspoon stevia
½ teaspoon monk fruit
2 tablespoon sugar substitute*
½ teaspoon salt
1 teaspoon vanilla

* See page 126 for sugar substitute options.

Tip: If you are using a metal cheese cake pan, wrap bottom and outside of pan with foil to help ensure the water will not leak into the crust. Whichever water method used, it will result in a creamier texture.

Option 1: To make "Turtle Cheese Cake", drizzle with "Caramel Sauce" on page 34 and "Chocolate Icing" on page 42. Top with chopped pecans.

Option 2: To make a delicious "Lemon Cheese Cake", blend in one teaspoon of grated organic lemon rind to cheese cake filling.

Blueberry Topping

This topping is perfectly paired with a lemon cheese cake. Topped off with a dollop of whipped cream, this makes a perfect dessert to end any meal.

....

In a medium saucepan over medium heat, combine maple syrup, lemon juice, arrowroot, sugar substitute, salt and stevia. Cook mixture until it starts to bubble and thicken. Turn down to low heat. Add blueberries and cook until it lightly bubbles and slightly thickened. Let cool to room temperature or refrigerate. When ready to serve, spoon topping over cheese cake. Add a dollop of "Whipped Cream Topping", page 93, if desired.

Note: This "Blueberry Topping" is the perfect complement to the "Lemon Cheese Cake", page 76.

¼ cup maple syrup
1 tablespoon lemon juice
2 teaspoons arrowroot
1 teaspoon sugar substitute*

⅛ teaspoon salt
⅛ teaspoon stevia
2 cups blueberries

*See page 126 for sugar substitute options.

PIES AND PUDDINGS

Apple Pie

Memories of autumn on the farm, Mom's apple pie cooling on the kitchen counter! Oh, that wonderful aroma of cinnamon!

Serves 6 to 8.

....

Prepare 2 unbaked pie crusts (see recipe, page 91).
Preheat oven to 375 degrees.
In a small mixing bowl, blend flour, sugar substitute, stevia, salt, and cinnamon. In a separate small mixing bowl, blend maple syrup and butter. Peel and slice apples. In a large bowl, combine apple slices and lemon juice. Place lemon coated apple slices in an unbaked crust. Blend dry ingredients into wet ingredients and pour over apple slices.

See special instructions for top crust on page 91.

Sprinkle cinnamon on crust. Bake at 375 degrees for 30 minutes. Reduce heat to 350 degrees for 30 minutes more.

Filling:

$\frac{1}{4}$ cup organic white flour
1 tablespoon sugar substitute*
$\frac{1}{8}$ teaspoon stevia
$\frac{1}{4}$ teaspoon salt
1 teaspoon cinnamon
$\frac{1}{2}$ cup maple syrup
3 tablespoons butter
6 medium apples
1 tablespoon lemon juice

Topping:

$\frac{1}{4}$ teaspoon cinnamon

*See page 126 for sugar substitute options.

Pecan Pie

This pecan pie is not overly sweet. It is just the right amount of sweetness that compliments the pecan crunch!

Serves 6 to 8.

Prepare unbaked "Pie Crust" (see recipe, page 91).

Preheat oven to 350 degrees.

In small mixing bowl, blend arrowroot or flour, sugar substitute, stevia, cinnamon, and salt. In a large mixing bowl, beat eggs and blend in maple syrup, butter and vanilla. Stir chopped pecans into wet ingredients. Add dry ingredients to wet ingredients. Pour mixture into an unbaked pie shell. Place pecan halves on top of pie filling. Bake for 40 minutes. (If the edge of the crust is getting too brown, cover the edges of the pie crust with aluminum foil 10 minutes before removing from oven.)

1 tablespoon arrowroot or white flour
2 tablespoons sugar substitute*
⅛ teaspoon stevia
½ teaspoon cinnamon
¼ teaspoon salt
2 eggs
⅔ cup maple syrup
¼ cup butter
1 teaspoon vanilla
1 cup pecans (chopped)

½ cup pecan halves (for top of pie)

*See page 126 for sugar substitute options.

Pumpkin Pie

At Thanksgiving, one thing I am thankful for is this healthy, low-glycemic pumpkin pie! Just as delicious as Mom used to make! Oh, and make sure there is plenty of real whipped cream to top it off!

Serves 6 to 8.

Prepare unbaked "Pie Crust" (see recipe, page 91).

Preheat oven to 425 degrees.

In a small mixing bowl, blend flour, cinnamon, ginger, nutmeg, cloves, sugar substitute, stevia and salt. In large mixing bowl, beat eggs and blend in maple syrup, pumpkin and half & half. Add dry ingredients to wet ingredients. Pour the pumpkin pie filling into an unbaked pie shell. Bake at 425 degrees for 15 minutes. Reduce heat to 350 degrees for 45 minutes more. Check with knife until it comes out clean.

Tip: **If prefer a more intense spice flavor in the pumpkin pie filling, increase cinnamon by ½ teaspoon and increase ginger by ¼ teaspoon.

1 tablespoon white flour

1 teaspoon cinnamon**

½ teaspoon ginger**

¼ teaspoon nutmeg

⅛ teaspoon cloves

1 tablespoon sugar substitute*

⅛ teaspoon stevia

½ teaspoon salt

2 eggs

⅔ cup maple syrup

1 (16 ounces) can pumpkin

¾ cup organic half & half

*See page 126 for sugar substitute options.

Blueberry Pie

Blueberry pie, topped off with vanilla ice cream, was another family favorite. I remember a time, when I was a little girl, traveling with Mom and Dad to the north woods to pick blueberries. I asked my mom if there were bears up there. When she said yes, I decided not to get out of the car. Needless to say, Dad was the only one picking berries that day; but later, we made the pie!

Serves 6 to 8.

Prepare 2 unbaked "Pie Crusts" (see recipe, page 91).

Preheat oven to 350 degrees.

In small mixing bowl combine flour, sugar substitute, stevia, cinnamon and salt. In a separate small mixing bowl, blend maple syrup and butter. In a medium mixing bowl, coat blueberries with lemon juice and lemon zest. Place lemon coated blueberries in an unbaked crust. Blend dry ingredients into wet ingredients and pour over blueberries. Bake for 45-50 minutes. Last 15 minutes cover with parchment paper to help thoroughly bake.

Filling:

¼ cup organic white flour

2 tablespoons sugar substitute*

⅛- ¼ teaspoon stevia

1 teaspoon cinnamon

¼ teaspoon salt

⅔ cup maple syrup

3 tablespoons butter

5 cups blueberries

2 tablespoons lemon juice

1 teaspoon lemon zest

*See page 126 for sugar substitute options.

Custard Cups

Custard is one of the most wonderful comfort foods. The creamy, smooth texture, along with the lightly sweet taste, just melts away the cares of the day!

Serves 5 to 6.

Preheat oven to 350 degrees.

In a food processor or large mixing bowl with mixer, beat eggs. Blend in maple syrup, sugar substitute, stevia, vanilla and salt. In a small saucepan, heat milk to very warm, but not hot. Slowly add milk into the remaining ingredients while mixing and blend well. Pour custard mixture into glass custard cups, filling the cup ½ to 1 inch from the top. Sprinkle nutmeg over top of the custard. Set cups in cake pan and place in the oven. Pour hot water around cups until water comes up to the level of the custard. Bake for 35-40 minutes, or until knife comes out clean.

Note: ***Grade "A" maple syrup has a thinner consistency and milder flavor than Grade "B" maple syrup. Using Grade "B" will result in a sweeter and more intense maple flavor.

Option: **For a richer flavor, replace 3 whole eggs with 2 whole eggs and 2 egg yolks. For a firmer mold (if removed from cup) or for custard pie, use whole eggs only.

3 eggs**
¼ cup maple syrup***
1 teaspoon sugar substitute*
⅛ teaspoon stevia
1 teaspoon vanilla
¼ teaspoon salt
1½ cups very warm whole milk

Sprinkle nutmeg (optional for on top)

*See page 126 for sugar substitute options.

Chocolate Cream Pie or Pudding Cups

Chocolate pudding topped with real whipped cream is one of life's greatest pleasures! Now even greater with this lower glycemic version.

Serves 6.

Prepare baked "Graham Cracker Crust", page 75, or baked "Pie Crust", page 91.

In small mixing bowl, combine cocoa, flour or arrowroot, sugar substitute, salt, and stevia. In a 10" to 12" fry pan on low heat, whisk honey, maple syrup and unsweetened chocolate until dissolved. Stir in milk until well blended. Add dry ingredients to wet ingredients. Blend with whisk and cook on medium heat until mixture thickens, about 20-30 minutes. Remove pan from heat at once. In a glass measuring cup, using a wire whisk, beat egg yolks with small amount of hot chocolate mixture. Slowly pour egg mixture into pudding mixture and stir rapidly. Over low heat, cook, stirring until very thick (do not boil) and mixture mounds when dropped from spoon. Remove the pudding from heat, stir in the butter and vanilla. Pour pudding into baking dish or pudding cups and let cool slightly. Cover with plastic wrap and chill in the refrigerator. When making chocolate cream pie, pour chilled pie filling into baked graham cracker crust or baked pie crust. Store the pie or pudding cups in the refrigerator. When serving, top with "Whipped Cream Topping", page 93.

1-2 tablespoons cocoa powder

¼ cup white flour or arrowroot

1 tablespoon sugar substitute*

¼ teaspoon salt

¼-½ teaspoon stevia

¼ cup raw honey

¼ cup maple syrup

1 square unsweetened baking chocolate
    (chopped fine or melted)

2 cups milk**

3 egg yolks

3 tablespoons butter

1 teaspoon vanilla

*See page 126 for sugar substitute options.

Tip: **Can substitute ½ cup, or all, non-dairy milk for dairy milk, if needed.

Note: When heating raw honey, use a candy thermometer to make sure the temperature stays at 140 degrees or below.

Option: To make a chocolate frozen treat, pour pudding in treat mold and freeze.

Banana Cream Pie or Vanilla Pudding

Another one of life's finest pleasures; creamy vanilla pudding and real whipped cream!   Top that! I will; with banana slices! A childhood favorite.

Serves 6.

Prepare baked "Graham Cracker Crust", page 75, or baked "Pie Crust", page 91.

In a small mixing bowl, combine flour or arrowroot, sugar substitute, stevia, and salt. In a 10" to 12" fry pan, whisk honey, maple syrup. Stir in milk until well blended. Blend dry ingredients into wet ingredients. Cook over medium heat. Using a candy thermometer, maintain temperature of 140 degrees, stirring until mixture thickens. Remove immediately from heat and set aside. In a cup with pour spout, whisk egg yolks with a small amount of hot milk mixture. Slowly pour egg mixture into fry pan with pudding, stirring rapidly to prevent lumping. Over low heat, continue cooking, stirring constantly until very thick (do not boil) and mixture mounds when dropped from spoon. Remove from heat, stir in butter and vanilla. Pour into a medium serving bowl or pudding cups, set aside to cool slightly.   Cover with plastic wrap. Chill in refrigerator. When making a banana cream pie, pour the chilled pie filling into a baked graham cracker or baked pie shell. Place banana slices on top of each piece of pie just before serving. Serve pie with "Whipped Cream Topping," page 93.

¼-⅓ cup white flour or arrowroot**

1½ tablespoons sugar substitute*

⅛ teaspoon stevia

¼ teaspoon salt

2 tablespoons raw honey

2 tablespoons maple syrup

2 cups half & half or whole milk

3 egg yolks

3 tablespoons butter

1-2 teaspoons vanilla**

2 bananas (sliced)

*See page 126 for sugar substitute options.

Note: Bananas can get brown and mushy if they stay inside or on top of the pie.   For this reason I add them prior to serving.

Options: **Use ⅓ cup flour or arrowroot and 1 teaspoon vanilla to make thicker donut filling and banana cream pie filling. Vanilla pudding will be a creamier consistency with ¼ cup flour or arrowroot and, if desired, 2 teaspoons vanilla for more flavor.

Rhubarb Custard Pie

When I remember my mother's baking, this pie comes to mind. It was one of my favorite pies, but I had to eliminate it from my diet because of the high content of refined sugar. Now I am happy to say, this naturally sweetened, low-glycemic version made it possible for me to enjoy it once again!

Serves 6 to 8.

2 tablespoons flour
⅛ teaspoon stevia
2 tablespoons sugar substitute*
½ teaspoon cinnamon
¼ teaspoon salt
3 eggs
2 tablespoons butter
¾ cup maple syrup
1 teaspoon vanilla
3 cups rhubarb (cut-up)

*See page 126 for sugar substitute options.

Prepare unbaked "Pie Crust", (see recipe page 91).

Make "Muffin or Pie Crumb Topping", (see recipe page 92).

Preheat oven to 325 degrees.

In a small bowl, combine flour, stevia, sugar substitute, cinnamon and salt. In a large mixing bowl, beat eggs and blend in butter, maple syrup and vanilla. Stir dry ingredients into wet ingredients. Stir in the rhubarb. Pour mixture into unbaked pie shell. Sprinkle crumb topping over pie filling. Bake for 1 hour.

Pie Crust & Gluten-Free Pie Crust

Testing, testing to find the perfect, mouth-watering pie crust! This one fits the bill! Flaky and buttery!

Makes 1 crust.

In a medium bowl, mix flour, baking powder, stevia, and salt. Mix in butter with a fork until crumbles are formed. Add milk and oil to the flour/butter mixture. Stir and form into a ball. Cover and chill in refrigerator for an hour. Transfer dough to pie plate and cover with plastic wrap.

Bottom crust:
Since pie crust crumbles easily, using your hand or bottom of measuring cup, push dough out until it covers the bottom and sides of the pie plate. Remove plastic wrap.

Top crust:
Roll out dough, set aside until filling is placed in the pie plate. When ready to cover pie filling, keep the top crust on the board, turn over the board, place on pie and slowly release dough from board with long surfaced spatula. Seal pie edges. Using a fork, poke holes in crust.

Lattice:
When rolling out lattice for top crust, roll between parchment paper. Place crust in freezer to harden. Once hardened, cut into strips, then remove with spatula. (To prevent from thawing when cutting and removing strips, place on a chilled surface. I used a flat cold pack). This will prevent them from breaking apart.

Tip: If you are using a glass pie plate, after forming crust to pie plate, hold it up to the light or window to see where you may have thin spots in the crust and fix as needed.

1 cup white flour
½ cup whole wheat pastry flour
⅛ teaspoon baking powder
⅛ teaspoon stevia
⅛ teaspoon salt
⅓ cup butter (softened)
1 tablespoon milk

3-3½ tablespoons oil (just enough to form a soft ball)

Gluten-free Pie Crust

1⅓ cups plus 2 tablespoons gluten-free rice flour blend
1 tablespoon oat flour
1 tablespoon buckwheat flour

⅛ teaspoon baking powder
⅛ teaspoon stevia
⅛ teaspoon salt
⅓ cup butter (softened)
1 tablespoon milk

3-3½ tablespoons oil (just enough to form a soft ball)

Pre-Baked Crust:
Set oven at 350 degrees. Bake for 20-25 minutes. Watch carefully not to burn. If needed, to keep from burning, cover with parchment paper last 5 minutes of baking. Cool before filling.

Muffin or Pie Crumb Topping

Makes approximately 1 cup.

In a medium mixing bowl, blend butter and maple syrup. In a small bowl, combine oatmeal, flour, sugar substitute, cinnamon, salt and stevia. Mix the dry ingredients into the butter and maple syrup mixture. Sprinkle a teaspoon of crumb topping over each muffin before baking.

Tip: * If using rolled oats, place in a food processor and chop to consistency of quick oats.

Note: If topping is too moist, place in freezer to firm the crumbles. Break up crumbles and sprinkle over muffin batter.

Option: Mixing in an additional 1 or 2 tablespoons of quick oats to the topping will also make it more crumbly.

1-2 tablespoons butter
1-2 tablespoons maple syrup
½ cup dry quick oats * *
¼ cup organic white flour
1 teaspoon sugar substitute *
¼ teaspoon cinnamon
⅛ teaspoon salt
⅛ teaspoon stevia

*See page 126 for sugar substitute options.

Whipped Cream Topping

Makes approximately 1 cup.

In mixing bowl, using electric mixer, beat cream, maple syrup, and vanilla until slightly thickened (soft peaks). If needed, to keep cream from separating, add cream of tartar while whipping and it begins to thicken. Continue beating until cream stiffens. Refrigerate.

8 oz. carton of organic cream

3 tablespoons maple syrup

½ teaspoon vanilla

¼ teaspoon cream of tartar (optional)

BEVERAGES

Creamy Hot Cocoa

On a cold winter's night, it's just nice to slow down, sit by the fire and watch a movie while sipping on this "I can't believe it's a healthy" cup of hot cocoa!

Serves 2.

2½ cups milk (dairy or your choice of non-dairy milk)

1 tablespoon plus 1 teaspoon raw honey

2 tablespoons cocoa powder*

¼ teaspoon salt*

⅛ teaspoon stevia

½ teaspoon vanilla

In a small saucepan, heat milk and honey. Add cocoa powder, salt and stevia. Whisk to blend. Heat cocoa until desired temperature is reached. Remove pan from heat and stir in vanilla.

Note: *Due to the fact different brands of cocoa powder vary in cocoa flavor, adjust cocoa powder and salt to taste. For desired sweetness, adjust honey and/or stevia to taste. A scoop of "Whipped Cream Topping" (page 93) and a sprinkle of cinnamon adds a nice rich flavor.

Naturally Sweet Lemonade

This was a big hit at a family baby shower! It is refreshing and oh so healthy too! It is a wonderful beverage for any party setting.

Serves 7.

In a drink pitcher, add honey and maple syrup to warm water and stir. Add and stir in lemon peel shavings, lemon juice, cold water, stevia, salt and ice cubes. Add lemon slices for garnish.

Note: If lemonade is too sweet, add more water to achieve desired taste.

Option: To make a quick and easy "0" glycemic lemonade, use 2 cups water, 2 tablespoons pure lemon juice and ¼ teaspoon stevia, or adjust sweetness to your taste.

¼ cup raw honey
¼-⅓ cup maple syrup
½ cup warm water
Lemon peel shavings
1 cup lemon juice (approx. 5 med. lemons)
4 cups cold water
¼-½ teaspoon stevia
⅛ teaspoon salt
Ice cubes
Lemon slices to float on top (optional)

Banana Split Smoothie

This is one of our favorite summer treats we enjoy sipping while sitting by the pool. A perfect way to cool down on those hot summer days!

Serves 4.

In a blender, add ingredients in the order listed. Blend until smooth.

1 cup milk (your choice)
1 cup "Homemade Ice Cream" (page 70)
1 frozen banana
½ cup frozen strawberries
½ cup canned pineapple (chilled tidbits or chunks)
½ cup juice from canned pineapple
Sprinkle stevia, to taste

Homemade Eggnog

Take a break during the busy holiday season. Sit down and relax with a cup of this delicious and creamy low-glycemic eggnog. Enjoy this new and improved festive creation!

Serves 4.

In a heavy saucepan, whisk eggs, honey, stevia and salt. Gradually add 1 cup milk. Cook and stir continually over low to medium-low heat until candy thermometer reads 140 degrees, approximately 20-30 minutes. Do not allow mixture to boil. Remove from heat immediately and transfer to a large bowl. Stir in vanilla, nutmeg and remaining milk. Place bowl in an ice water bath, stirring until mixture cools. After mixture cools, remove from ice water bath. Cover and refrigerate until cold, approximately 2 to 3 hours. After cooled, beat cream until soft peaks form. If desire more sweetness, add 1 to 2 tablespoon of maple syrup to cream just before soft peaks form. Whisk whipping cream into eggnog mixture. Sprinkle eggnog with additional nutmeg before serving, if desired.

Note: Be careful eggnog does not get too hot and keep stirring or it may curdle. When serving, dilute with milk if prefer a thinner consistency or desire less sweetness.

3 eggs
¼ cup raw honey
⅛-¼ teaspoon stevia
⅛-¼ teaspoon salt
2 cups whole milk (divided)
1½ teaspoon vanilla
¼ teaspoon nutmeg
½ cup heavy whipping cream

Fruit Punch Concentrate

A refreshing fruity punch packed with healthy whole fruits and juices! If you want more added flavors, unsweetened flavored sparkling water will do it!

Makes 6 to 8 (½ cup servings).

In a food processor, blend all the ingredients in the order listed. Pour into glass jar and store in refrigerator or freezer until ready to serve. For a single serving, pour equal amounts of "Fruit Punch Concentrate" and sparkling water, stir to blend. If using a party punch bowl, pour all of the fruit concentrate into bowl, add approximately 3-4 cups sparkling water, to taste.

Option: To add more fruit flavor, double the amount of strawberries and add one tablespoon of honey or add according to taste. If too thick, add more water or juice.

2 tablespoons lime juice
2 tablespoons lemon juice
1 cup fresh or frozen whole strawberries
½ cup pineapple chunks (canned)
2 cups pineapple juice
2 tablespoons raw honey
2 tablespoons maple syrup
⅛ teaspoon stevia
Sprinkle of salt (optional)

Sparking water, unsweetened (added when serving)

Cola Syrup

On a quest to find a healthy, low glycemic soda drink, I realized there was virtually nothing out there to fill that need. I formulated a healthy syrup that could be added to carbonation, for an alternative to the usual sugary or chemically sweetened soda.

Serves 4.

In medium saucepan, combine the syrup ingredients. Bring this mixture to a boil on high, lower the heat to medium-low and simmer uncovered for about 10 minutes. Turn heat down to low and continue cooking until flavors blend, for about 20 minutes. Remove the syrup from heat and cool. Use a small strainer to filter the citrus zest from the syrup. Store in a glass jar in the refrigerator. When ready to serve; blend 2 to 3 tablespoons of "Cola Syrup" with sparkling water to taste.

Option: Cherry Cola - In a small glass cup, add 1 teaspoon of black cherry tea leaves. In a tea kettle, boil ¼ cup water. Add hot water to the black cherry tea leaves. Cover and steep for 15 to 30 minutes. Cool and strain. Add 1 to 2 teaspoons black cherry tea to the cola drink, according to taste. Add sprinkle of stevia, if needed, and stir. Flavored tea can be found on-line or at your local tea store.

1 lemon (juice & zest)
1 lime (juice & zest)
2 oranges (juice & zest)
1 (5 inch stick of cinnamon, broken in 2 pieces)
1 teaspoon cinnamon
1 teaspoon coriander
¼ teaspoon nutmeg
½ cup maple syrup
⅛ teaspoon stevia
½ teaspoon vanilla
Sprinkle of salt (optional)

Sparkling water, unsweetened (added when scrving)

Ginger Ale Syrup

Fresh ginger gives this ale a natural bite. It also has a nice citrus flavor that compliments the ginger.

Serves 4.

In medium saucepan, add ginger and water. Bring to a boil on high. Lower heat to medium-low and simmer uncovered for 20-30 minutes. Watch carefully so that the water does not evaporate completely. May need to cover sooner or reduce cooking time. If needed, add small amount of water. Turn off heat, cover and let steep for 15 minutes. Take out ginger pieces and discard. Add lemon juice, lime juice, maple syrup, honey and stevia. On medium-high, heat this mixture until the temperature reaches 140 degrees. Reduce heat to medium, maintaining temperature while simmering. Stir occasionally. Lower heat to medium-low and cook down to blend flavors, about 10-15 minutes, until consistency of real maple syrup. Remove from heat and cool. Pour into a glass jar and store in the refrigerator. When ready to serve; in a drinking glass, blend 1 to 2 tablespoons "Ginger Ale Syrup" with sparkling water to taste.

½ cup fresh ginger (peeled and chopped)
1 cup water
¼ cup lemon juice
2 teaspoons lime juice
¼ cup maple syrup
1 tablespoon raw honey
⅛ teaspoon stevia
Sprinkle of salt (optional)

Sparkling water, unsweetened (added when serving)

Root Beer Syrup

If you need a quick pick-me-up; natural root beer, made with black tea, will do it! It is also a refreshing change from the overly sweet or chemically sweetened root beer drinks we are so familiar with.

Serves 1.

In a small glass, add loose tea. In a tea kettle or small saucepan, boil water. Pour boiled water into the glass of tea leaves. Stir tea, cover and let steep for at least 15 minutes, or more for a richer flavor. Place tea in refrigerator to cool. Strain loose tea from liquid. Throw away the loose tea leaves. In a medium to large glass, add strained tea, blend in maple syrup, stevia and vanilla. Add sparkling water to taste.

Tip: If prefer more sweetness, sprinkle additional stevia or add a small amount of maple syrup, to taste. Enjoy immediately.

Note: You can find flavored teas on-line or at your local tea store.

1 teaspoon black tea with sarsaparilla
½ cup water
1 tablespoon maple syrup

⅛ teaspoon stevia
Splash of vanilla
Sprinkle of salt (optional)

Sparkling water, unsweetened (added when serving)

Ginger & Raw Apple Cider Vinegar Drink

I have found raw apple cider vinegar helps with my digestion when taken with meals; especially heavy, hard to digest meals. I had to come up with an easy recipe I would enjoy drinking. Adding ginger adds a wonderful flavor and helps with digestion. It has a nice fizz as well. If you have acid reflux or an ulcer, be cautious when drinking raw vinegar, as for some people, it can irritate the stomach lining.

Serves 1.

In a glass, add all ingredients and stir.

6-8 oz filtered water
1 teaspoon raw apple cider vinegar
⅛ teaspoon ginger powder
Sprinkle stevia, to taste

Green Protein Smoothie

I enjoy this smoothie every day! It's a great pick-me-up in the morning and mid-afternoon! I never tire of this wonderful and satisfying drink! It's a tasty meal in a glass!!

Serves 1.

In a blender or smoothie maker, add ingredients as listed. Blend until smooth. Drink immediately.

Tip: *Freeze fresh spinach by placing it in a plastic gallon zipper bag, press out the air to vacuum seal. After freezing, crush frozen spinach in the bag. Store bag of spinach crumbles in freezer.

Option: Add a handful of blueberries for extra anti-oxidants. For a tropical smoothie; add mango, pineapple, and papaya (good for digestion).

½ cup cold water
½ cup milk (your choice)
3 tablespoons protein powder
⅛ teaspoon stevia
1 cup fresh spinach or ¼ cup to ⅓ cup
    frozen crushed spinach*
¼ frozen banana
2 frozen strawberries
1-2 teaspoons flaxseed meal and/or chia seeds
Sprinkle of salt (optional)

BEVERAGES 109

Cinnamon Turmeric Tea

Turmeric is known to have anti-inflammatory properties. The addition of the cinnamon adds a nice flavor and has been known to stabilize blood sugar levels as well. This tea is one I like to sip on throughout the day.

2 cups boiling water
½ teaspoon turmeric
⅛ teaspoon cinnamon
Pinch of black pepper (for absorption)
Sprinkle stevia, to taste

Makes 2 cups.

Boil water in a medium pan or teapot. In a glass quart jar, add the turmeric, cinnamon and black pepper. Pour hot water into the jar and stir. Steep for approximately 10 minutes. Let cool and sprinkle stevia to taste. Store in refrigerator. Serve hot or cold.

Option: When cooled, add milk (your choice) for a creamier consistency.

Caution: Turmeric may stain fabrics.

Chai Tea Latte

Many of us enjoy a flavorful Chai Tea Latte as our morning pick-me-up! Unfortunately, along with flavor, it is very high in sugar. With this new lower glycemic version, it still contains plenty of flavor and just the right amount of sweetness to satisfy!

Serves 1-2.

Chai Tea Syrup: In medium saucepan, bring water and spices to a boil. Turn off heat, add tea bags, cover and steep for 5-7 minutes. Remove tea bags, squeezing out excess water and flavor from tea bag. Discard tea bags. In a glass jar, using a fine strainer, pour and strain tea. Add honey, vanilla and stevia. Set aside to make latte or place in refrigerator until ready to use. Store in refrigerator up to two weeks.

Latte: In medium saucepan, heat milk and honey just until steamy, not boiling, using candy thermometer to maintain temperature of 140 degrees or below. If desired, add a light pinch of stevia and stir. Remove from heat. Using a hand blender, blend milk mixture to a frothy consistency. Pour ½ cup of chai tea syrup into a warm mug, slowly add 1 cup of frothy milk. Sprinkle with a pinch of cinnamon, if desired.

Chai Tea Syrup:

2 cups water

⅛– ¼ teaspoon cloves

1 teaspoon cinnamon

½ teaspoon ginger

½ teaspoon cardamom

½ teaspoon nutmeg (optional)

⅛ teaspoon salt

⅛ teaspoon pepper

2 bags black tea (spiced chai)

1 tablespoon raw honey

½ teaspoon vanilla

⅛ teaspoon stevia

Latte:

½ cup "Chai Tea Syrup"

1 cup organic whole milk

1 teaspoon raw honey

Pinch of stevia (optional)

Pinch of cinnamon (optional)

SALAD DRESSING
AND SAUCES

Sweet & Salty Vinegar Oil Dressing

Sweet and salty salad dressings have always been a favorite of mine, but the original recipes contain a lot of sugar! Since I didn't want to give up my sweet and salty salad dressing, I desperately needed to find a replacement for this wonderful taste sensation. I began to experiment with ingredients I had in my refrigerator to find the perfect flavor combinations to replace my favorite dressing. What a wonderful blend of flavors!

Makes approximately 1 cup.

....

In a medium bowl, whisk ingredients until well blended or in a shaker, add ingredients and blend. Store dressing in the refrigerator. Pour dressing over salad, toss and taste until you reach the desired amount of flavor.

Tip: For a different variation: Add chopped apples with or with-out skin. Add or replace sunflower seeds with walnut pieces.

Option: *Replace 1 tablespoon of apple cider vinegar with 1 tablespoon balsamic vinegar for a nice change of flavor.

½ cup oil (your choice)
2 tablespoons of raw apple cider vinegar *
2 tablespoons maple syrup
1 teaspoon original blend seasoning (salt-free)
½ teaspoon lemon pepper (salt-free)
½ teaspoon onion granules
¼ teaspoon garlic granules
⅛ teaspoon stevia
⅛ teaspoon salt

Salad Ingredients:

Chopped iceberg lettuce	Chopped spinach
Chopped onions	Shredded carrots
Shredded cheese	Real bacon pieces
Sunflower seeds	

Creamy Coleslaw Dressing

The "Sweet & Salty Vinegar Oil Dressing" is also a great coleslaw dressing. Adding mayonnaise helps the dressing cling to the shredded cabbage. The celery seed is optional; although, it does add a nice complimentary flavor.

Makes ¾ cup.

In a medium mixing bowl, whisk "Sweet & Salty Vinegar Oil Dressing" and mayonnaise until well blended. Pour over shredded cabbage, add to taste.

½ cup "Sweet & Salty Vinegar Oil Dressing" (page 114)

⅓ to ½ cup mayonnaise

¼ teaspoon celery seed (optional)

14 ounce bag of coarsely shredded cabbage

Peanut Dressing

"Peanut Dressing" adds a nice rich flavor to fruit and vegetable salads. It is a very simple recipe that can be whipped up in minutes!

Makes 1 cup.

In food processor, puree all ingredients. Store dressing in refrigerator until serving. Pour over spinach, shredded carrots, walnuts pieces and chopped apples, then toss.

Caution: Be aware of those who have peanut allergies before serving.

½ cup oil (your choice)

¼ cup raw apple cider vinegar

2 tablespoons raw honey or maple syrup

½ teaspoon salt (or less, if desired)

⅛ teaspoon stevia

¼ cup peanuts

Ketchup

Ketchup also contains a lot of added sugar. Now using this lower glycemic version, our favorite condiment can be a healthy addition to the meal.

Makes approximately 2 cups.

2 (6 ounces) tomato paste
½ cup water
⅔ cup distilled white vinegar
⅔ cup maple syrup
 1 teaspoon salt
½ teaspoon onion granules
¼ teaspoon garlic granules

In a small saucepan, on low to medium-low heat, using whisk, blend ingredients. While using candy thermometer to maintain temperature at 140 degrees or below, simmer ketchup for 10-15 minutes. Stir occasionally. Cook until desired sweetness. Note: The more it cooks down the sweeter it will be. Remove ketchup from burner and cool. Pour into pint glass jar or ketchup bottle, cover and store in refrigerator.

Note: Add ½-1 tablespoon of raw honey for a richer flavor. Adding honey will increase the sweetness, reduce maple syrup to ½ cup. If ketchup becomes too thick, then add 1 or 2 tablespoons of additional water until desired consistency. This option is recommended for no-bake use only.

French Dressing

French dressing was one of my mom's favorite dressings. It has a wonderful sweet and tangy flavor, but again, it contains a large amount of sugar. Here is the same great taste without all that sugar!

½ cup oil (your choice)
½ cup "Ketchup" (page 117)
¼ cup maple syrup
¼ cup vinegar
1½ teaspoons onion granules*
1 teaspoon paprika
½ teaspoon salt
⅛ teaspoon mustard powder
⅛ teaspoon stevia

Makes approximately 1½ cups.

In a medium mixing bowl or shaker, blend all ingredients as listed. Serve over favorite salad ingredients. Store dressing in refrigerator.

Note: *Salad dressings will not keep as long if they contain fresh onion. For this reason I only use onion granules in my salad dressing recipes. If you prefer smoother dressing, use one teaspoon of onion powder.

Option: Add ½ teaspoon Worcestershire sauce for a nice added flavor.

BBQ Sauce

My husband loves this BBQ Sauce on his slow-cooked venison. Tastes just like a pulled pork BBQ sandwich with a kick!

Makes approximately 1½ cups.

In a small saucepan, combine all ingredients as listed. Stir together until well blended and simmer on medium-low heat for 5-10 minutes. Pour into glass jar, cover and store in refrigerator until needed.

Glazing:

Use spoon or basting brush to coat baked or slow-cooked chicken or ribs. Place barbecued meat in oven at 350 degrees or under broiler until glaze is baked onto the meat. Watch carefully not to burn sauce.

Note: If using a slow-cooker to make hot beef or venison, stir in desired amount of BBQ sauce after meat has finished cooking and falls apart. This BBQ meat is also great eaten without bread, along with a side of macaroni and cheese!

Option: If you like hot spice, add a pinch of cayenne red pepper or jalapeno.

1 cup "Ketchup" (page 117)
2 teaspoons yellow mustard
¼-⅓ cup "Date Paste" (page 66)
¼ cup maple syrup
2 tablespoons soy sauce
1 tablespoon molasses
1 teaspoon liquid smoke or mesquite spice
1 teaspoon chili powder
1 teaspoon onion granules
¼ teaspoon salt
¼ teaspoon garlic granules
¼ teaspoon pepper
Sprinkle of stevia (optional)

BBQ Hamburger Sauce

Another familiar name for this sandwich is a "Sloppy Joe". The name I often give my self, because it is so true, I am the original sloppy Jo!

Makes approximately 2 cups sauce for hamburger.

In a medium mixing bowl, combine all ingredients listed, except hamburger and celery. Add sauce to fried hamburger and cook with one stalk of celery, cut in half (take out after cooking) or if you like celery, add one celery stalk (chopped) to the sauce ingredients. Simmer on low for approximately 15-20 minutes to blend the flavors and slightly thicken sauce.

Note: If sauce is too thick, add approximately ½ cup water.

Tip: *If possible, use organic tomato soup with less than 10 grams of sugar per cup.

¾ cup organic tomato soup*
   (not condensed)
¼ cup water
1 cup "Ketchup" (page 117)
1 tablespoon Worcestershire sauce
2 teaspoons raw apple cider vinegar
2 teaspoons yellow mustard
2 teaspoons onion granules
½ teaspoon garlic granules
Salt and pepper, to taste

1 pound fried hamburger and finely
   chopped onions
1 stalk celery

Quick Baked Bean Sauce

Baked beans are always a nice addition to summertime picnics. Oh, but we sure don't need the addition of MORE sugar! Here is a quick, low-glycemic version to the traditional sugary sweetened baked beans we love.

Makes approximately 2 cups baked beans.

In a medium saucepan, combine all ingredients, except for the beans. On medium heat, stir the sauce mixture until well blended and begins to simmer. Turn heat down to low. Add beans to sauce and let simmer for 10-15 minutes to incorporate the flavor of the sauce. Turn off heat and leave saucepan on burner until it cools. Place in refrigerator overnight or serve immediately.

½ cup "Ketchup" (page 117)
2 tablespoon water
2-3 tablespoons maple syrup, to taste
½ tablespoon molasses
2 tablespoons bacon pieces (bottle or crispy fried)
1 teaspoon onion granules or powder *
⅛ teaspoon dry mustard (optional)
¼ teaspoon salt
⅛ teaspoon pepper
Sprinkle of stevia (optional)

One 15 ounce can pinto or navy beans drained.

Tip: *Add ¼ cup chopped onions (saute or replace with onion powder for a smoother sauce).

Note: It is best to marinate overnight to allow flavors to absorb into the beans.

Option: To make baked bean casserole, add ½ pound fried hamburger, and if you desire, swap out one cup of pinto or navy beans for kidney beans. Can also double recipe and replace with two other types of beans, such as great northern beans and butter or lima beans.

Cocktail Sauce

To my surprise, cocktail sauce is quite sweet. I realized I needed to add this condiment to my collection of low-glycemic recipes!

Makes 1¼ cups.

In a small bowl, combine all ingredients and stir until well blended. Serve with shrimp. Store the cocktail sauce in the refrigerator until ready to use. Throw out any leftover sauce that was used for dipping.

1 cup "Ketchup" (page 117)
2 tablespoons lemon juice
4 teaspoons horseradish
½ teaspoon Worcestershire sauce

Creamy Tartar Sauce

A fish fry is not complete without the perfect tartar sauce. When I decided to make my own tartar sauce, I was surprised to find out how sweet it is. This sweet and tangy tartar sauce, without refined sugar, is the perfect condiment for the next fish fry!

Makes approximately 1 cup

¹⁄₃ cup chopped dill pickles (no juice)
1 tablespoon minced onion *
1 tablespoons lemon juice
½-1 tablespoon raw honey
Very light sprinkle of stevia
1 cup mayonnaise

On a cutting board, cut one medium dill pickle in half. Cut a piece of onion, equal to one tablespoon. In a food processor, finely chop dill pickles and onion. Add in lemon juice, honey and stevia, continue processing. In a small bowl, combine mayonnaise, ingredients from the food processor and stir until well blended. Store tartar sauce in refrigerator until serving.

Note: *Some brands of mayonnaise might have a thinner consistency than others; because of this, I have included variations to adjust the thickness of the sauce. For example, replace chopped onion with ½-1 teaspoon onion granules.

Cranberry Sauce

Cranberries are very tart and require a lot of sugar to make the cranberry sauce! When changing from refined sugar to natural liquid sweeteners, I found they blended nicely with the citrus flavors in this favorite side dish. No refined sugar needed here!

Makes approximately 2 cups.

In a medium saucepan, using whisk, blend first 8 ingredients until smooth. Add cranberries. Using candy thermometer, heat to temperature 140 degrees. Stir occasionally. When cranberry sauce begins to simmer, turn the heat down to low. While maintaining temperature of 140 degrees, continue simmering for 10 minutes. If using a cinnamon stick, remove it after cooking and discard.

Option: For less sweetness, reduce honey and maple syrup to ¼ cup each. Taste to check for sweetness. If need more sweetness add sugar substitute of your choice.

½ tablespoon sugar substitute*
⅓ cup maple syrup
⅓ cup honey
⅛ teaspoon stevia
½ cup fresh squeezed orange juice
1 teaspoon orange zest
1 teaspoon lemon zest
1 cinnamon stick or ½ teaspoon cinnamon
2 cups fresh or frozen cranberries

*See page 126 for sugar substitute options.

SUGAR SUBSTITUTES are part of the formula that replaces refined sugars in these recipes. I've chosen chicory root fiber sweetener and date sugar for their well-researched health benefits. To see how to incorporate these two sweeteners together into your recipes, refer to page xxiii, Option #3. To order chicory root fiber sweetener on-line, search "zero sugar baking sweetener chicory root fiber" so not to be confused with the coffee substitute, roasted chicory root powder.

CHICORY ROOT FIBER SWEETENER is keto-friendly, prebiotic fiber that promotes digestive health and may lower insulin resistance. Per teaspoon it contains 0 grams sugar, 3 grams carbs/0 net carbs, 3 grams fiber and 3 calories. It blends nicely into all the recipes and has a pleasant taste like cane sugar.

COCONUT SUGAR: Be careful when choosing other sweetener replacements for those used in "Treat Your Health", such as coconut sugar. It looks good on low-glycemic charts, but since it has been concentrated to a dry form of sugar, it has the same amount of calories and carbohydrates as refined white sugar. If you prefer to use coconut sugar, especially for children, I suggest keeping the amount very low and adjust according to taste. Example for the "Peanut Butter Cookies" or the "Chocolate Chip Cookies": add 2 tablespoons to ¼ cup coconut sugar, reduce the maple syrup in this recipe by one measurement and replace 1-2 tablespoons of fiber sweetener with 1-2 teaspoons fiber sweetener. This small amount should be well tolerated, but if not, then omit this sugar substitute.

DATE SUGAR is a low glycemic, fiber-rich superfood; for example, it's rich in nutrients such as potassium. Although it is rich in fiber, it may be gentler on the digestive tract than sugar alcohols or chicory root fiber sweetener. Date sugar works best in moist chocolate cake or spice cake and muffins due to the date flavor and fiber content. I found it does not work well in sugar cookies, butter cookies, or chocolate chip cookie dough, making them crumbly and changing the flavor profile. Since it does not dissolve well in liquids, it is not recommended for beverages.

OTHER ZERO SUGAR SUBSTITUTES are available to choose from. For example, allulose is a keto-friendly option. The taste and texture is similar to sugar. It's 70% as sweet as sugar, so may need to use slightly more, to achieve the right amount of sweetness in these recipes. Since a small amount is found in such foods as figs, raisins, and kiwi, most mass-produced allulose comes from corn. On-going research is being done for safety and health benefits. Research is showing small amounts are safe to use. Per teaspoon it contains 0 grams sugar, 4-5 grams carbs/0 net carbs, 0 fiber, and 0 calories. Since it   closely resembles cane sugar, it should incorporate well into all recipes. Since keto-friendly sweeteners have become more popular, there may be more healthy options to choose from as research continues.

Note: All the recipes in this book were created using only chicory root fiber sweetener as the sugar substitute. When using sugar substitutes other than chicory root fiber sweetener, the recipe may require more liquid if too dry or more flour if too wet depending on what other sugar substitute chosen.

REFERENCES

COOKBOOKS

- *Sweet and Natural*, by Meredith McCarty. New York: St. Martin's Press, 1999.

- *Smart Bread Machine Recipes*, by Sandra L. Woodruff. New York: Sterling Publishing Co., Inc., 1994.

- *Nature's Sweet Secret*, by David Richard. Vital Health Publishing, 1996.

WEBSITES

- *Nutrition and You* - www.nutrition-and-you.com

- *Medicine Hunter* - www.medicinehunter.com

- *Organic Facts* - www.organicfacts.net

www.ingramcontent.com/pod-product-compliance
Lightning Source LLC
Chambersburg PA
CBHW041832110726